"Profession and Beyond"

M SIVA RAM PRASAD

First Published in February 2022

ISBN: 978-93-5472-728-3

BLUEROSE PUBLISHERS

www.BlueRoseONE.com

info@bluerosepublishers.com

+91 8882 898 898

Cover Design:

Muskan Sachdeva

Typographic Design:

Rohit

Distributed by: BlueRose, Amazon, Flipkart

Dedicated to
My wife Rama Devi
And
My sons Sai Thejasvee and Tapasvi
who have been travelling with me
in this journey.

INSIDE OUTSIDE

NOT A GREAT IDEA

There is nothing new about writing an autobiography. Similar works are written by people from many walks of life. However, these works can be divided into two distinct subcategories; the ones written in the middle age and the ones written after the active life. The writings in the middle age propagate the person and his activities. The writings after active life, on the other hand, describe the experiences and reminiscences. My attempt belongs to the second category.

What was so great about my life? I always used to be in a dilemma whenever somebody asked me that. Why should I write my story at all? Friends like Dr N Bhaskar Rao and Alok Kaul from New Delhi persistently asked me to write the story only because my professional life was not on a beaten track. I know it is difficult to write even about a professional career without divulging the secrets. Now, this is the case for any biographer. Unless one is interested in raising eyebrows and creating temporary controversies, if not contemporary history.

The storytelling invariably revolves around me and my life but what interest it creates in the minds of the readers especially when it is not meant for a particular category of readers. With no intention to boast, the work is an effort to explain the self and above self.

I always thought that a biography should convey a message; not necessarily explicit. It is left to the reader and his judgement. What difference would it make if the work is never published? This question always lingers in my mind.

There is not much to talk about my life except my profession. Nevertheless, I tried to make it interesting by narrating relevant history, wherever needed. It is for you to judge. I am sure you will like what I wrote between these lines.

I thank my son Sai Thejasvee who spent time in reading my first draft, giving suggestions and correcting it.

I thank my assistants Mr. Kancherla Sri Ram, Mr Vilekh Bachu and my office manager Sri Polipilli Appa Rao who have helped me to turn this book into reality.

I am grateful for all those who stood by me and made me who I am today.

I thank my wife Rama Devi, my sons Sai Thejasvee and Tapasvi who have been with me in this entire journey and helped me with their cooperation. I dedicate this book to them.

Roots and Genes

"The origins are from an educated and liberal thinking background. Comfortable living in a rural environment made a lot of difference in understanding the realities in life. This helped in sustaining uncompromising principles that I believed. The inspiration and thought process, I got from the genes are deep-rooted. The roots I developed I am sure will be spread and some of the thoughts."

Where to start the story, especially when everything seems like a quick flash of light in front of my eyes? I have to travel seven decades back to narrate the story of my life. I was born on 17th April 1951 in a port town of the East Coast, Machilipatnam, situated in Andhra. This is a small town that has not grown over centuries but was a launching pad for Portuguese, Dutch and French nationals who traded with the Indians in earlier centuries. French ceded the place to the British in 1759 who opened their agency in 1611.

Our Village

I come from Repalle Taluk in Guntur district which is also close to the East Coast. My village is Vellaturu in Repalle Taluk. Close to our village, river Krishna's rivulet passes through and after about 10 kilometres reaches the Bay of Bengal. Our village has a history of its own with a few rare temples like Vinayaka where two of his consorts Siddhi and Buddhi, *Kalyanam* (marriage) is conducted and a chariot is drawn on *RathaSaptami* day every year. The popular belief was that Vinayaka is a bachelor, who makes our temple unique. . It was built approximately in the 15th or 16th century. A stone, engraved with some information regarding Indian medicine, was found on the premises. There is another temple called Agastheeswara which is considered to be installed by the Sage Agastya and it is supposed to be one of the five *shivalingas* established by him. Another Temple is for Chenna Keshava, which is also a rare temple. Additionally, there is a temple for Shiva and Tripura Sundari. These sprawling temples are well laid out. Our family donated for the establishment of Sri Sharada Peetham by Sringeri Shankaracharya. On this occasion, Shri Shankaracharya visited our house and performed some sacred rituals in our *pooja* room. He later addressed the public who had gathered from different villages to see him in our compound.

The distance between Vellaturu and Bhattuprolu, the nexus of Buddhist history in South India, was only three kilometres. The stupa was considered to be built in the 2nd century BC, which is earlier than Amaravati.. Ever since the stupa was ransacked and looted, there remained only a round shaped mound, a few hundred words in the history books that mention a golden and a crystal casket which were used to preserve Buddha's relics.. The stone edict found in this place is one of the many remains, marking the origin of Telugu language script. It is also considered to be the basis for South Indian language scripts including ancient Tamil as per Dr Tirumala Ramachandra in his book '*Mana Lipi Dani Puttu Purvottaralu*'. Bhattiprolu was under the Mauryan and

Gupta Empires, which was then known as Pratipala Puram. The stone edict located in Bhattiprolu belongs to the pre-Ashokan period and the script that was found had been developed and changed in different dynasties in later centuries. The irony is that the stones removed from the stupa were used in building the Vellaturu lock in our canal system in the later part of the 19th century and building a bridge on the sluice canal near Bhattiprolu on Vellaturu road according to Alexander Rea.

Our village is situated in a highly fertile area where farmers have been growing paddy, turmeric, black gram, green gram, Bengal gram, *mirchi*, and fruits. Canal irrigation is available from Krishna canals, which is enough to grow three crops.

Parents and Family

I come from an agricultural family with a substantial landholding. My grandparents Moturu Sri Ramulu Garu and Lakshmi Devi passed away in the same year when my father Shri Ankineedu Garu (1911 – 1988) was five years old and my aunt Anasuya Devi (1916- 1992) was six months old. They were raised by their grandmother Srimati Tirupatamma and the properties were managed by my grandmother's sister Varalakshmi Devi's husband Nagabhushanam Garu who was also the first cousin of my grandfather Sri Ramulu Garu. We followed a Hindu joint family system, even though the properties were divided and identified. Father at a very young age inherited 42 acres of fertile lands.

The village had a middle school up to 8th standard as early as 1900, which later adopted an education system known as the basic education system, propagated by Gandhiji by the time I had already studied in the same school. My father received his education up to 8th grade in our village and then in Kolluru up to SSLC (11th class) which is five miles away from our village. Kolluru is famous for finding Kohinoor diamond. If you visit the mouth of Krishna river in the rainy season, you might find some diamonds and other precious stones even today.. During the British regime, mining was extensively done to find diamonds in the river mouth and the adjoining areas. After his education was completed at Kolluru, he moved to Machilipatnam for his higher education where he graduated from Noble College. It was the only first grade college in the entire Andhra area which was part of Madras Province, offering a degree level education.

He proceeded to Calcutta University for doing his Masters in Commerce (1932-34) which was not taught in South India at that time. His Vice Chancellor was Shyama Prasad Mukherjee, son of great Asutosh Mukherjee. Shyama Prasad was the founder of Janasangh, a political party, which later merged into Janata Party that became Bharatheeya Janata Party (BJP). He was also a minister in Nehru's interim cabinet in 1946. Sri G Basu who was teaching commerce in the Calcutta University, became a president of The Institute of Cost Accountants of India in 1959,was also a president of The Institute of Chartered Accountants of India. He was my father's professor at Calcutta University. Calcutta at that time was the capital of India where the governor-general was stationed.. In 1931, however, the British made New Delhi the capital of India and completed the shifting processes from 1932 to 1934. He was the first postgraduate in Repalle Taluk. He was planning to go abroad for his foreign education. Due to the onset

Author's Father Sri M Ankineedu

Author's Mother Smt Syamala Devi

of the Great Depression, the economy was shattered, and he changed his ideas of going abroad.

He got married to my mother Syamala Devi (1915-1992), daughter of Boppana Somayya Garu, a railway contractor from Krishna district settled in Tenali. Her mother Kokila Bai was from Bilaspur in old Central Provinces, which is presently situated in Chhattisgarh State. Her maternal great grandfather Ammanna Garu migrated from Pedamaddali in Krishna district to the Central Provinces. He and her grandfather Naganna Garu undertook military transport contracts, railway and road contracts in Nagpur, Kamptee and Bilaspur.

My mother's maternal uncle,Kokila Bai's elder brother, Dr Edpuganti Raghavendra Rao was not only one of the early barristers in the country (1910 – 1914) but also the Prime Minister of CP and Berar 1927- 30, chief minister in 1937 and governor in 1936 of Central provinces and Berar(the present Madhya Pradesh, Chhattisgarh and parts of Maharashtra). If that was not enough, he also became the adviser to the Secretary of State in London between 1939-1941 and was a member of the Viceroy's Executive Council with Civil Defence portfolio up to June 1942.

My mother who had studied up to matriculation (Nagpur), was a trained singer, a well-read person and a great disciplinarian.

Her mother, Kokila Bai had two sisters and all three of them were trained by an English governess. They were taught Telugu by Shrimati Bandaru Achamamba, a famous Telugu writer in those days and sister of great historian Sri Komarraju Lakshman Rao Garu. The elder sister of Kokila Bai, Shrimati Ramanujamma was a regular contributor to *Hindu Sundari*, a Telugu literary magazine. She also published a book in 1922 "*Putropaharam*" which constituted letters to her son on culture, education, etiquette etc. Nehru's letters to his daughter were published eight years later. The younger sister, Tripuramba Garu had translated the history of England into Hindi as " *England Ki Kahani* ". What's interesting about them is in those days women were not allowed to go outside the house. Nevertheless they were educated at home, resided in a non-Telugu state while continuing their pursuit of Telugu and coming to Andhra area after marriage.

My grandmother used to tell us that before their marriages in Andhra, they worked as volunteers in Congress. "We were in no way less than Vijayalakshmi Pandit but societal and community restrictions in Andhra did not allow us to participate in public life". They compared themselves with Vijaya Lakshmi Pandit because she too was not formally educated. Additionally, her brother Dr E. Raghvendra Rao was one of the contemporaries of Motilal Nehru, who had co-founded Swaraj Party, along with *Desa Bandhu* Chittranjan Das. She once told me that Lokmanya Tilak used to stay as her father's guest in their house in Kamptee and Bilaspur. Under some extraordinary circumstances, both Pandit Ravi Shankar Shukla and Srimati Rajendra Kumari Bajpai were given political asylum for a couple of months by my grandparents at Tenali. If Srimati Rajendra Kumari Bajpai wouldn't have revealed this to Sri E Ashok Rao, son of Dr E Raghavendra Rao , the secret would've been lost forever in the depths of time. Sri Ashok Rao also served as a cabinet minister in Madhya Pradesh (1993-1998).

My mother had four siblings, Indira Devi, Kamla Devi, Sarda Devi and Rajasekhar Rao. In addition, two of her first cousins Kausalendra Rao, son of Ramanujamma Garu and Kutumba Rao, son of Ramaiah and brother of Somayya Garu also grew up along with them in Tenali, till completing their college education and professional education. They all lived like one family.

Kausalendra Rao Garu went to England for higher studies at the London School of Economics after his graduation from Pachaiyappa's College in Madras. He did his barrister and was a member of Lincoln's Inn in the year 1934.After his return, he practiced at Nagpur High Court and became advocate general at the age of 36. Later, at the age of 39, he became High Court judge and achieved a record-breaking feat in India. He became a member of the first finance commission, which has laid down the principles of sharing revenues between the centre and the states. He was the senior-most judge next to Sri M Hidayatullah, the Chief Justice in the Nagpur high court.

Kutumbarao Garu was a successful lawyer at Vijayawada and a director of Andhra Bank, president of Bezawada Bar Association for the Diamond Jubilee year and associated with many social organisations and educational institutions. He was married to the daughter of Rao Bahadur Kovelamudi Gopala Krishnayya Garu, an advocate and member of Madras Legislative Council (1921) and an author of couple of books including *Principles and Methods of Taxation*.

Moturus

Father was dissuaded from moving out of the village for education since he was the only male child and can manage the properties, but he continued his education in spite of the pressure and odds he faced. The family, especially his grandmother, looked after and followed him till his graduation at Noble College, Machilipatnam. Nagabhushanam Garu was educated up to high school. He passed Hindi exams as a qualification to get a post in the Congress hierarchy. He participated in the freedom movement and was jailed twice during the Civil Disobedience movement and Salt Satyagraha. He served as a member of the district Congress Committee. He wore Khadi and supported Congress throughout his life.

The other side of his life was also interesting. He was a member of Chennapuri Andhra Mahasabha and enjoyed going to horse racing as a punter to Madras, Bangalore, and Bombay. I have a letter written by him from Bombay asking my grandmother to hand over his gun to revenue authorities who will come and collect it on a specific date. He also used to go for a shoot. He served as the president of the Vellaturu panchayat for a number of years without contest .The village significantly developed under his tenure. My grandfather lived in a luxurious lifestyle by getting his clothes stitched in Madras. He also had a collection of walking sticks, overcoats, footwear, and was a connoisseur of food and drinks.

Contrarily, my father, in spite of having higher education in Calcutta, was leading a simple life with high thinking. He was associated with Dr Ram Manohar Lohia during those days. One of his cousins, Moturu Radha Krishna Murty, a postgraduate from the same university worked with Dr Ashok Mehta, another socialist leader as a research assistant a few years later. Dr Ashok Mehta became Deputy Chairman of the Planning Commission when Nehru was Prime Minister. With his education and association, father became cardholder of the Communist Party of India. However, he relinquished it in the late 1960s. I remember as a child when people discussed about him as a candidate for one of the two delegates from India for an International Conference in Germany. Unfortunately, he was not permitted due to his affiliation with a political party. His service records were seized and the issue was raised in Andhra assembly. My father was a good orator who was adept in translating speeches of Dr Harindranath Chattopadhyay when he was contesting for Lok Sabha from the Vijayawada constituency. When Teachers Federation proposed his name as a candidate for the Member of Legislative Council (MLC) 1962-63, he refused on health grounds and proposed the name of Sri P Sri Ram Murthy instead and supported him. He became MLC for three terms. The first election meeting was conducted by my father.

I observed both my grandfather and father and followed the best from both in my life.

My grandmother Varalakshmi Devi (1902 -1989) was also educated in Telugu and Sanskrit. She was skilful enough to read the scriptures and explain. She had beautiful handwriting. I have a couple of letters written by her to my mother. Not only that, but she was also a highly religious person, who devoted most of her time to performing *pooja* and reading scriptures. She was practicing to maintain purity, called *Madi* in Telugu in the house.. The couple had no children .They treated my father and his sister as their children only. My father implicitly obeyed them without any question, as he would to his parents. My mother and I also followed the same.

Our ancestral house in the village, where my father was born, was the biggest in the village. It was also the witness to an enervating great famine from 1876 to 1878 (*Dhata* year as per Telugu calendar and known as *Dhata Nama Karuvu*) and a couple of devastating floods. My grandfather had tastefully built a house in 1949, which was away from the village and located on the main road leading to Repalle in agricultural land of 2.5 acres with the raised platform to protect from snakes and other animals. It had a coconut garden with a sprawling cattle shed, storehouse for agriculture produce etc. The village was gifted with electricity in the year 1961- 62. We had a pump set for watering the agricultural land and also the residence. The village is close to the railway station by about two kilometres. The bus facility was available from Tenali and Repalle.

It is a well-connected village with wireless facility and is centrally located to have administrative control on villages, especially during the Krishna River floods. When canal transport was popular, large boats used to come for passenger travel as well as goods transport. Water levels of the canal were controlled and the lock was functioning for efficient canal water management and the transportation of boats. It also constituted a middle school and high school which are not normally found in a village. It had its travellers' bungalow. These facilities existed from the pre-independence days. Later, grandfather had built a rest house for senior officers as a donation, who used to come for inspection on the request of the government, where his portrait was unveiled..

We also donated for constructing a bus depot building with a night halt facility, and veterinary hospital in the name of grandparents. An additional donation was made for building one floor in the High School on the existing administrative block. The family has donated for renovating the Ramalayam and given an endowment for establishing *Sringeri Sharada Peetham* in our village. Philanthropy has been a part of our family tradition.

Moturu is a village near Gudivada in Krishna district but most of the Moturus are found in Vellaturu Guntur district probably because of migration. This migration is generally facilitated due to the existence of a direct road between Gudivada to Potharlanka, a village close to Vellaturu during Buddhist days as per G Jouveau-Dubreuil in his foreword to the book *Buddhist Remains in Andhra*. Some of the Moturus can be found in Komaravolu village in Krishna district. The Moturu clan was initially associated with agriculture but after the introduction of English education, they were identified as well educated. This is the first surname from Andhra with which there were two Rajya Sabha members; one was Moturu Satyanarayana Garu, famous for his propagation of Hindi in South India through Dakshin Bharat Hindi Prachar Sabha. His son Pratap Kumar, a chartered accountant, was my senior in Madras. Another famous person from the clan was Shri Moturu Hanumantha Rao Garu, a former editor of *Prajasakti* the popular Telugu daily and the organ of the Communist Party Marxist in Andhra. My father was senior to Hanumantha Rao Garu.

Life in the Village

Life in village had been really interesting during those days because of its connectivity and several infrastructural and transportation facilities were very close to Tenali, an important railway junction on Madras-Delhi, Madras-Kolkata route which was known from the days of MSM Railways (1916). In addition, a loop line between Repalle and Guntur was in operation as early as in 1920 and Bhattiprolu railway station was also located 3 kms away from our village. Civilization, education, culture, and agriculture made life very interesting. Every modern facility that existed during that time was available at our house. Occasionally, I would visit orchard and other agriculture fields with escorts of course, to watch the harvest processes and to understand it in detail. Watching the rising and receding flood levels from the flood control Bund known as *Kara katta* and participating in religious functions in temples was exciting. In this prosperous and rich village, it was really difficult to find the trace of poverty in people. *Thirunaal* (sacred day)festival added exuberance to the village for two weeks.. It was celebrated by conducting a trade fair for articles produced by artisans, carpenters, weavers and others, before and after the *kalyanam* of Lord Vinayaka. For watching the latest movies, father and I used to go to Tenali.

All types of seasonal fruits were grown in our own garden because grandfather was keen on growing them and enjoyed eating.

Living in the village was no less luxurious and exciting than living in any urban area with all the modern amenities covered. The absence of hustle and bustle of urban life, was a cherry on the cake.. We used to get *Indian Express* and *Andhra Patrika* for my father and grandfather. *VisalAndhra* the organ of Communist Party of India was another Telugu daily regularly subscribed. In addition, two Telugu weeklies for grandmother, *Andhra Patrika* and *Andhra Prabha* which were read by a majority of the women in the house. We had also subscribed to two spiritual magazines for grandmother, *Yadardha Bharathi* and *VedantaBheri*. My father used to regularly subscribe to Himmat of Rajmohan Gandhi, *Organiser* of Balraj Madhok, *Blitz* of RK Karanjia and *Swarajya* of C Rajagopalachari. Mother had subscribed to *Margadarsi*, a health magazine.

Each one of us used to have our own brand of toothpaste like Macleans, Forhans, and Kolynos. Soaps like Margo, Lux, Mysore sandal, and Necko. Beverages like Ragotine were saved for me, Planters Coffee Propaganda (PCP) coffee for grandfather and my mother, Brooke Bond Red Label tea for father, Ovaltine or Bournvita for grandmother. My grandfather used to get Amla hair oil from Bengal chemical works by postal parcel.

I am compelled to mention these details because what is talked of consumerism as of now, we have been enjoying that 60 years ago in our village. Only electronic gadgets, computers and cell phones are additions now.

Perhaps that is why JK Galbraith in his book *Affluent Society*, told Pandit Nehru the Prime Minister that the standard of living in Punjab is better than some of the southern states in the USA. Krishna delta specially Tenali- Repalle area was no less in this aspect. All the enviable affluence is due to the development in agriculture induced by the development of irrigation canals by Captain Alexander Rea in 1890 and Sir Arthur Cotton before that. In addition to that, advancement in higher education was facilitated with the development of village high schools and colleges as early as 1920. As per statistics, the undivided Guntur district had the highest number of high schools as a district in the entire country. Tenali revenue division had the highest revenue collection in the Andhra State.

The area between Tenali and Repalle, extending up to Nidubrolu has produced enlightened, educated and civilised people of national and international recognition. Scientists like Dr Y Nayudamma (Yalavarru), his Guru Katragadda Seshachalam (Inturu), doctors like Dr Kolluru Venkata Rayudu (Mulpuru), Dr Vulakki (Tenali), both were educated at Edinburgh. Justice Avula Sambasiva Rao, chief justice AP High Court (Mulpuru), leaders like N G Ranga (Nidubrolu), Moturu Hanumantrao (Vellaturu), Makineni Basavapunnaiah (Turpu Palem), Vemulapalli Sri Krishna (Bethapudi), KCP ltd group founder Sri V Ramakrishna ICS (MineniwariPalem). Film personalities like Lakshmi Rajyam (Tenali), S Janaki (Repalle), producer and director Chakrapani from (Itanagaram), Hero Krishna (Burripalem), director K Visvanath (Pedapulivarru). Literary personalities like Tripuraneni Gopichand (Tenali) and Tummala Sita Ramamurthy (Kavooru), the author of *Andhra Prashasti*, are only a few names which I am mentioning here. It is a great inspiration to know about them, who have come from a rural background and received education in this region which led them to such heights in an era where many areas in the rest of the country were struggling for basic needs.

LITERACY AND EDUCATION

"Literacy is only a tool for learning but education is a continuous process. I am still a student on a daily basis, the profession I am wedded to, compels me to learn and update. Life makes me understand the people and situations."

School and College

I had been moving along with my parents in childhood since my father was the headmaster of Zilla Parishad high schools in Krishna district, Andhra Pradesh. He used to work as headmaster of ZP High School in Addada where my *akṣharabhyasam* (initiating the formal education) was performed. It took place in 1955. My mother was not present since her brother Kausalendra Rao Garu was ailing and in comatose in Nagpur. My father did not want to lose time. So I was formally sent to the elementary school. The total strength of the school was about 50. There were only two rooms in the entire school. Sometimes, in summer, classes were conducted under the Banyan Tree nearby. Before I joined the school, I was taught at home. My mother taught many *slokas* in Telugu and Sanskrit. I completed my education upto class three there. Later, on my grandfather's request,, I did my class four in our native village. It was a school with a basic education system propagated by Gandhiji where the students participated in keeping the school clean and conducting weekly assemblies where they used to act as ministers. I was an education minister for a few months. Craftworks like carpentry and weaving were also taught as part of the curriculum. From class five to seven, my school education continued in Kothuru TadePalli near Vijayawada. However, later we had to move back to Vellaturu on grandfather's request, asking my father to involve and manage the properties, agricultural activities and horticulture due to his increasing age. For three more years I studied at Vellaturu High School. Again, we moved to Krishna district as my father was supposed to work for one year before his retirement to reap retirement benefits.

I studied SSLC (class 11) in a place called AaruTegala Padu near Kaikaluru. The request and pressure came from the people of Tadepalli through Kakani Venkata Ratnam Garu to post father in Tadepalli again. The people from Arutegalapadu wanted my father to continue so a lot of pressure was mounted on the Zilla Parishad chairman, Sri Pinnamaneni Koteswara Rao through Kamineni Peda Venkayya Garu. The chairman of Zilla Parishad often wondered as to who is this great teacher that is preferred by people and why hadn't he never come across him. Then he came to know that my father was actually the son in law of Boppana Somayya Garu. The chairman's father Sri Veeraiah Garu and my grandfather Somayya were first cousins. Despite all of this, my father was never interested to influence anyone in his career. He felt that his services are required by people of all corners and never used to seek favour or a particular posting. To seek no favours, was a lesson taught to me by my father through his actions.

I was always a class topper in my school up to SSLC except in mathematics

An eleven plus one system was followed during that time. I opted for science in my pre-university course. Sri CVN Dhan, my father's student accompanied me to Andhra Christian College in Guntur and took me straight to the principal, Sri J Paulus and got the admission. Sri Dhan was a well-known teacher and principal of Ravi Tutorial College (later Ravi college), famous for discipline as well as teaching and success of the student. I was surprised to see him standing with folded hands for a long time when both my parents visited him at his house. That was his devotion to my parents. He was my godfather in Guntur. When we visited him, he invited Sri A S Raman, editor of *Illustrated Weekly* of India for dinner where he narrated the story of leaving *Amrita Bazar Patrika,* due to certain differences with Deva Das Gandhi on editorial policy. This narration made me inquisitive about journalistic freedom and editorial policy.

For one year of college days, he did *guru puja* and honoured my parents in a large meeting. After completing my pre-university course, I wanted to do B. Pharmacy, because during that time basic drugs were in short supply in the country. I dreamt of inventing a medicine like *Amrutanjan* which was a popular balm for pain relief, colds, and headache. It was and still is a household medicine for everyone which was regularly purchased by many people along with groceries. It is used by people irrespective of age. However, I could not secure a seat in pharmacy owing to cutthroat competition.

My father was not in favour of repeating the exam for upgrading my score. He suggested that commerce is better option for students like me. He knew that I was not going to excel in science due to the competition. He explained to me that once five-year plans are completed, there will be growth in business and industry which will spike the need for finance and management people His predictions soon turned into reality.

I was admitted in Hindu College Guntur, as it was the only college teaching commerce at that time. Again, Sri C V N Dhan accompanied my father and I and took us to Sri YSR Chandran, the principal of Hindu College and got me admitted. I was never a first class student in college, but I did participate in several quiz programmes, which resulted in one-year captaincy of the quiz team. Our team won many competitions consistently for three years in Andhra Loyola College Vijayawada and was successful in retaining the cup for our college. I also learnt the German language through the classes conducted by Max Muller Bhavan. I can say that in college, through attending a majority of political and spiritual meetings and paying regular visits to American library, I sought for practical knowledge.

CA Training

Father knew how I studied and he was not very keen when I wanted to do CA after my commerce graduation. He thought that I was not a serious and hardworking person. So, he asked me, 'are you capable of passing the course like CA?'. I took it as a challenge and said yes. I sought the help of my maternal uncle Kutumba Rao Garu to get a seat in Brahmayya & Co. in Madras for my apprenticeship. It was difficult to get a seat because of the limited number for training. He spoke to Mr Brahmayya on phone and arranged the seat. They both used to call each other Bava (brother in law in Telugu) and he wrote a letter mentioning that, "He is my sister's son and son of the second daughter of Somayya Garu". Brahmayya Garu received me with affection and inquired about the family members. Sri Mallikarjuna Rao, son-in-law and nephew was also a partner in the firm. He was also the nephew of Shri Parvata Neni Bhushaiah Garu, a former member of the legislative council of Madras (1926) and husband of Shrimati Annapurnamma Garu, my mother's elder sister in the undivided family of Boppanas.

I was registered as an audit clerk with a training period of four and half years. I was committed to my job and did good audits of Easun engineering, VST Motors, Lucas TVS, Sundaram Finance, The Hindu, Madras Motor and General Insurance Company and United India Insurance Company. Both the insurance companies were later nationalised.. I gained a lot of experience from the work I did there and the help I received from my seniors. There used to be nearly 60 article apprentices headed by a dozen paid chartered accountants and about 40 paid staff with six partners.. In such a cosmopolitan atmosphere, my outlook widened. Only in the last leg of a few months, I shifted to Guntur due to health reasons.

I excelled in the CA examination without many failures in 1977. I used to see a board in the Church on Nungambakkam High Road near our ICAI office saying, 'JESUS NEVER FAILS'. One student who struggled to get through the examination wrote on that board, "LET HIM APPEAR FOR CA". I felt immense satisfaction of winning the challenge and proving myself to my father.

I enjoyed learning and doing work as an articled assistant. It helped me in my practice in later years especially in audits. Whenever I visited a factory, I tried to understand the manufacturing process, its raw materials, components, and other inputs. This helped me in understanding the industry. Not only that, but it also aided me in preparing project reports while rendering corporate financial consultancy services. I never took my training as a routine or my learning as an effort to get qualified as a chartered accountant. I was always taught that the purpose of education is to understand the situation, its needs, and to assimilate the essence of everything you observe, listen, read or practice and apply the knowledge to solve the problem.

After my graduation at the age of 19, going to a conservative state for a tough course made me more disciplined, systematic, and stronger. Those were the real formative years in terms of my professional life because I saw there rich children of big businessmen working hard and being humble. That was really the steppingstone of future life in profession.

Education at Home

Whatever I described above only forms a part of my literacy. My earliest education started at home with Panchatantra stories and Aesop's fables. For making me learn the essence of morals, my mother used to quote one of the famous sayings of Vidura from *Mahabharata*, 'Wealth, education and family background make persons with bad temperament arrogant and those with good temperament, humble'. This made me a person without complex thinking. My father always used to explain about the general economy and Indian economy in particular and how it works. He also used to explain me about land, labour, capital, and organisation. He used to say, ' Agriculture in India is a gamble with rains.'

Living in villages and witnessing the lives of people from close quarters was a great education and practical training in life. My grandfather refused the proposal of sending me to Rishi Valley School. He asked my parents, 'Do you think he will get a better education than what can be taught by you both at home?' Grandmother used to read *Mahabharata* which was serialised in *Andhra Patrika* in the Sunday issue and explain most of its discourses, which revolved around an analysis and discretion between *dharma* and *adharma* (righteousness and wickedness) . Such readings moulded my personality along with improving literacy and gave me real education.

Coming from a background where my father was a staunch leftist, a grandfather with freedom fighting experience, grandmother's religious approach and mother's aristocratic family background gave me an overall perspective of life. Setting up practice and struggle for proving myself made me realise what life is.

I always remembered Nehru's message from jail to Indira Priyadarshini on her eighth birthday. "Fear is a bad thing and unworthy of you, be brave and all the rest follows".

"Grow up as a child of the light, unafraid and serene and unruffled whatever may happen".

I always followed this maxim in life.

Being a strict disciplinarian she is, my mother was interested in the development of my overall personality. My father, being a liberal and often said, "Both Marcus Aurelius and Chesterfield brought up their sons with a lot of care but the sons were not up to the expectations". Perhaps he never wanted my mother to get disappointed. Reading in general, updating on current affairs, improving writing skills, appreciating music and art was mainly because of my mother and her initiatives. She taught me how to behave, speak softly and avoid hurting other's feelings.

My father was a man of convictions and modern thinking who always tried to think different than the majority. He always said, ' Public opinion is an ass; it is this public opinion that gave poison to Socrates".. Not only that, but he also told me to not have a 'mass mentality' and asked me to read, *Unpopular Essays* by Bertrand Russel. During discussions on religion and its practices, he used to say, 'There is more irreligion in the name of religion in this country' and used to quote Tolstoy saying that, 'He was interested in Christianity and not in Churchianity.' He never shied away from expressing his aversion to practices that are not founded on fundamental principles. By the time I became a CA, I had understood that philosophy is like the objects clause of a company and religion is like the articles of association of a company under the Companies Act. I used to attend the lectures of Arya Samaj Guru Pandit GopaDev in Guntur during the evenings and listen to Thiruppavai in the mornings during the month of January. Arya Samaj propagated Vedic religion but Thiruppavai is based on Puranic religious practice. I was inquisitive about both. Ultimately parents trained me in understanding the rationale behind everything in a country where rations were being imposed for basic food grains, sugar, kerosene etc. For me, everything was food for thought and was shaped up as a nonconformist with a positive attitude for learning and creativity.

LIFE IN PROFESSION-CREATIVITY AND STRATEGIES

"Starting the profession at a time where development was the buzzword with nationalisation philosophy and restrictions were imposed on foreign investments with thrust on indigenisation, which gave courage to the Indian enterprise. The environment encouraged creativity and more opportunities."

I started my professional life over four decades ago, in 1977. After passing chartered accountancy, I only wanted to practice and that too in the capital city of undivided Andhra Pradesh, Hyderabad. The opportunities were more in the city and the atmosphere for industrialisation was ripe, with the spike in the growth rate of small and medium scale sectors. When I landed in Hyderabad, I didn't know even it's roads. I was attracted to the opportunities in financial consultancy, preparation of project reports, conducting feasibility studies and counselling before financial institutions and banks. My experience in industrial audits, audit of banks and state-level financial institutions encouraged me in pursuing the tasks.

Initial Struggle and Challenges

I was 25 when I actually started my life. When I say life, I mean life in profession and I was one of the youngest to start my professional life in those days without inheriting the professional practice from parents or family. The initial years were tough.

When I passed out, my father gave me the freedom to choose my professional path. However, he did caution me that I'll have to struggle initially and advised me to be strong enough to withstand the stress and strain and not look back. I followed his advice. It was really a struggle for the first five years. Making both ends meet was difficult. Being the only child, with a financially well-to-do background, it is needles to mention that my father always supported me financially whenever required.

I relocated from Madras to Hyderabad. Shri Pulugurta Venkata Subba Rameswara Prasad (PVSR Prasad) was my roommate in Madras for three years. We became very good friends and wanted to practice together. I did not join his firm since the proposal was to start office at Vijayawada.

Shree Manthena Achyuta Rama Krishnam Raju (MARK Raju), a common friend and slightly senior to both of us was practicing at Raju and Raju Chartered Accountants, a proprietary firm and he wanted me to join him as a partner. After prolonged discussions, I joined him as a partner in 1977 and both of us started Raju and Prasad in 1979, exclusively for private sector works. We practiced together up to 1985-86 and parted our ways to take over one firm each. Mr S. Ranganathan joined me as a partner in 1985. I have expanded Raju and Prasad in New Delhi, Mumbai, Bangalore, and Jalgaon. In the biannual survey by the

Prime Academy in 2018, the firm ranked 208 in a sample of 2000 firms in the entire country. We have gone a long way in this journey and achieved many milestones.

Picking up work for a new entrant in the profession was difficult. My friends from Madras, Sri Panuganti Ramu, a chartered accountant and Shri Gadiyaram Udaya Bhanu helped me in getting some work for verifying accounts and finalising the balance sheet of small firms. Later, they helped me in getting into Babu Khan Business Enterprises as an auditor since their advisor Mr Abdul Razaq, a chartered accountant and advocate, was practicing mainly as advocate and had appeared in Income Tax Appellate Tribunal and High Court. Later Mr Razaq became a member of the Income Tax Appellate Tribunal. We became their auditors. Both Mr Basheeruddin Babu Khan (later a Minister in Sri Chandrababu Naidu's cabinet) and his brother Mr Ghayasuddin Babu Khan were kind and I continued as their auditor for a number of years. The brother-in-law of Ghayasuddin Babu Khan, popularly known as Khurshid Sahab, Jagirdar of Bidar started a steel re-rolling mill Hy Steels Pvt ltd, at Kadthal on the way to Srisailam. He made me the auditor of company and continued as such till it changed hands to a Marwari firm. He liked my work and recommended as auditors of a company from Bidar. I was told that Sri V S Kaujalgi, who later became speaker of Karnataka Assembly and Shri B D Jatti, who later became Vice President of India were interested in being the promoters of the company. I used to visit Bidar for auditing purposes and advising the board on Company Law matters. This was our first work outside Andhra Pradesh.

Shri Panuganti Ramu also introduced me to Mr Byron Fernace proprietor, of J.C Pinto Book Stores and director of Mekaster Tools Private Limited. This company was importing critical tools and equipment and supplying the same in India. He was another client who supported me in the initial years and proposed my name in 1979 as a member of Secunderabad Club. Byron introduced me to Capt. P L Uniyal, another engineering equipment supplier and we continued as auditors. Captain Uniyal introduced me to Mrs Usha Bharat Singh, who along with two other Army officers was in the process of setting up a manufacturing company for making security alarms. That was the first start-up company I took up where we successfully continued to render our services.

None of my clients in the initial years shared my caste, region, or language. It was my conduct, competence, and winning manners that made me survive in Hyderabad. I enjoyed the cultural amity and religious harmony of the city. It suited my upbringing and cultural background. Built on the foundations of friendship, my life continued.

After about a year of practice, I asked my parents for money to buy a car. My mother told me, 'Buying a car is not a big deal but never get accustomed to any comfort unless you are sure of maintaining the same throughout your life.' I always kept that principle in mind for the rest of my life. Another maternal uncle Sri Boppana Rajasekhar Rao Garu, a top executive of Brooke Bond India, who worked in Madras at that time selected a car for me. It was a two-door, sparingly used Herald car. Interestingly, it was one of the three cars owned by the General Manager of Indian Oil Corporation. My uncle purchased it for Rs 5850. The price of petrol then was only Rs.3 per litre. I repaid the car money later. My cousin Suresh and I drove the car from Madras to Hyderabad.

Getting a branch audit of the bank for a young, chartered accountant like me was impossible, if it wouldn't have been for my maternal uncle Sri Bopanna Kutumba Rao, long-standing Director (nearly 13years) of Andhra Bank and a popular advocate.. During those days, the bank had only 400 branches; where each auditor received 20 branches at the fee of Rs. 400 per branch including the expenditure.. The total fee of 8000 rupees was considered great for a beginner. There was no gain but it was a prestigious work. All the branches were from Kurnool district and I drove in my car along with my cousin Suresh and one assistant.

One day while travelling from Nandyal to Srisailam, the car was unable to pull in the ghat section due to lack of engine oil. We had to stop the vehicle and put engine oil. When we got down from the car, we realised that we were in the midst of Nallamala forest at 9 in the night. With nowhere to go, I was really scared of the wild animals that could be wandering in the forest for food. It was a very frightening experience.

Expansion of Activities

The profession of chartered accountancy observed slow growth, but I felt that there is tremendous potential as the country was progressing industrially and financially. My father's prediction of growth in the country after the implementation of five-year plans came true, and need for management and finance professionals picked up. Taking this into consideration, I took the challenge of practicing as a chartered accountant. To combat the slow growth and expand our activities, I had broad-based the firm and registered with the Comptroller and Auditor General of India (C and AG), RBI, and other National and state-level institutions. During those days, a majority of professionals associated with tax representation and tax appeals.

Andhra Pradesh was carved out after linguistic state formation and it had limited resources. Metropolitan cities like Mumbai, Kolkata and Madras had a specific industrial and business culture since a century.. Although Hyderabad was the fifth largest city in the country, it was a bit late in cultivating an industrial culture, probably owing to its identity as a princely state and landlocked.

While broad basing the firm with more professionals and branches, I always kept Sri Parvathaneni Brahmayya, founder of Brahmayya and Company, as a role model where I was trained as an apprentice for CA in Madras. He was a highly respected person in this profession and was one of the earliest chartered accountants trained in England and Wales in the 1930s.

Public sector and private sector

Although we have started with considerable professional work with public sector undertakings, they were not remunerative for the effort, time, and risk taken by professionals. But there is always a feeling of prestige for professionals in those years. Commercial audit done by chartered accountants is always reviewed by the Comptroller and Auditor General of India (C and AG). It is not only a review but, C and AG also used to comment on the accounts of these undertakings. Sometimes these comments can be damaging to the auditing firm. We sought the advice of a senior chartered accountant Shri A. Ramachandra Rao for precautions to be taken to avoid any adverse comment.

After gaining experience in a couple of years, I always believed that the commercial audit done by chartered accountant and propriety audit done by AG are supplementary and complementary. The scope and purpose of audit and the related opinion expressed are different in all respects. I continued this approach in my four decades of audit practice during public sector undertakings. Statutory auditors' role is totally different. They have to express their opinion on the fairness of the affairs of the auditee whereas government audit looks into propriety of the transactions. Whenever there was any suggestion for any improvement in my presentation and disclosure, I always accepted and implemented them in the next year, especially when they were given by government auditors. However, I never easily accepted for change in the signed accounts.

Maintenance of accounts by Central Public Sector undertakings is always good. They always followed the manual meticulously which was prepared even before the commercial operations. Our experience about the maintenance of accounts in state government undertakings is far from satisfactory. The remuneration for these assignments is low even today, considering the cost of services and value of the time of senior professionals.

We continued our stint in public sector undertakings in spite of low revenue earning and only valued the recognition at the National level by C and AG and other National level Regulators.

Private Sector works

Simultaneously, I was looking for work in the private sector also. One of my early clients was Sri G.V Rajasekhar, whose father was secretary to RTA Shri GV Krishna Reddy. Rajasekhar wanted to set up a bus body building unit. He was a young engineer and decided to be a technocrat. We incorporated a company in the name of Bhagyanagar Body Builders Private Limited. Today, the company has grown to the level of number one bodybuilders in the private sector after Hyderabad Allwyn. Related to this case, I had won an interesting appeal in income tax on the definition of manufacturing. Income Tax Authorities were not willing to give certain deductions and incentives as a manufacturing company since it is only bodybuilding. The contention of the department was manufacturing means producing a product but the definition is to convert any material into another product of different commercial use. I quoted number of cases where making food and making clothes out of cloth was also considered manufacturing. This is a case of making an ordinary chassis as a bus for passengers which is covered as per the definition. My appeal was decided favourably.

The group expanded to manufacture toughened glasses to be used in automobiles with Swedish Technology. In South India, this was the first toughened glass unit after ATUL in Gujarat. I had also won an interesting appeal on the taxability of Technical Services by foreign technicians. The foreign technicians visited India to install the plant and machinery to commence , commercial production and prove the rated capacity of production. The payment for their services was separate as per the agreement which has to be paid in foreign exchange with RBI's approval.

Department contended that the services are not technical in nature. However, I opposed based on the definition as per the Income Tax act. I won the appeal. That was how my stint with tax work started successfully, even though I never had any specific training in tax work.

My friendship with them continues till today, even though both the companies were taken over by bigger players at that time. Rajasekhar was always curious to search for new products for the automobile industry supported by his brother Shree Vijaya Raghava. I always used to exchange my views on automobiles and its components due to my exposure in audits of TVS group in Padi Industrial Estate Madras.

Shri MJ Rao, a general manager of Tata Electricals, who graduated from Banaras Hindu University, and post-graduated from Illinois Institute of Technology advised his sons-in-law, Shri G Narayana Rao and Sri GKB Chowdary to give work to my firm. Both of them started taking our services from 1980 and continue till date. Both Shri Narayan Rao and Chowdary had best business practices and are honest in compliances and tax payments. They both have grown into two business groups, Orchem industries and Vasant chemicals. It was always challenging yet pleasurable to work with them as an advisor.. They would always be ready to fight on any matter of dispute with tax authorities and never compromised on principles. It always gave us the comfort since I shared a similar mindset and our firm also stood for certain best practices in the profession since inception.

Corporate Financial Consultancy

I always felt that there are many services that can be rendered by a chartered accountant and not necessarily the traditional tax work and auditing. There were other areas like advising on Foreign Exchange Management Act (FEMA), foreign direct investment, identifying new projects, preparation of detailed project reports with technical inputs, recruitments, financial planning, equity advice etc. I felt the need for consultancy for many entrepreneurs who were setting up new industries and the late 70s was the time for development of industries in Andhra Pradesh.

Dr Marri Chenna Reddy inaugurated the Jeedimetla Industrial Estate and gave a call for the development of industries in Hyderabad. I was one of the invitees for the meeting by a group of young entrepreneurs who started ancillary industries to APSRTC. Later, Sri J Vengala Rao, another chief minister continued the spirit and developed Patancheru Industrial Estate for the large-scale sector. George Fernandez emphasised the need for mass production by the masses. That was how the beginning of industrial development in SME sector started in Hyderabad.

I visualised the future industrialisation in the state and believed it to be a consequence of Faridabad Congress resolution to introduce economic reforms like the new deal of Roosevelt in USA by Mrs Indira Gandhi, who won by one vote of Sri Sadiq Ali as majority. The emphasis was to provide employment, ensure availability of finance from banks and financial institutions to technocrats.

The banks and insurance companies were nationalised. New breed of entrepreneurs came into existence, the SME sector was developed and some of those entrepreneurs became major industrialists. Andhra Pradesh was in the lead for starting AP State Financial Corporation (APSFC), AP Industrial Development Corporation, (APIDC), and AP Small Scale Industries Development Corporation (AP SSIDC) which was followed by other states. Shri Ram K Vepa an IAS officer was the Pioneer in the concept of SME and started the concept of Development Financial Institutions at the state level.

Today, the concept of development has taken a backseat and instead, liberalisation has encouraged the selling of the institutions. Private sector undertakings started the thinking of exit route, which was not there for major groups like Bajaj, Mahindra, TVS, Tatas, Birlas, and Kirloskars, but the new generation of entrepreneurs think of quick money without any attachment with the enterprise. Government thinking is still worse compared to new entrepreneurs, who wants to sell the public sector undertakings for a song. The revenue on the sale of public sector undertakings has become a part of the source for the annual budget of the country. This is like selling family silver to meet the daily bread and butter of the country.

The policymakers and bureaucrats are advised by foreign consultants who have no attachment to this country and are working under the influence of vested interests. The country is being sold in different ways economically and culturally. It seems ironical that our country got independence with the slogan *Swadeshi*, which is now being replaced with the slogan, *videshi*. Anything *videshi* is great, be it a razor blade or a luxury car.

Pradhan Management Consultants Pvt ltd

I feel that I have digressed a bit from developmental financial institutions. Knowing the direction of industrialisation, I started Pradhan Management Consultants in 1982 with Shri M Dhananjay, a friend of my father, an industrialist and director of AP SSIDC. He was very knowledgeable about the industries, especially the SME sector.. The purpose behind this was to provide consultancy services to start-ups. The new technocrats cannot afford to have full-fledged offices or have knowledge on various corporate laws. They also don't know how to get the number of clearances from various government agencies. Through our services, we could help a few people who were setting up ancillaries to major industries, but were somehow unable to make great strides. One of the major projects was a 100% export-oriented unit (EOU) to manufacture l-cysteine from human hair. This was the first 100% EOU in Andhra Pradesh which was established near Tirupati at Mangam Pet Industrial Area, with technical collaboration of a Japanese company with 100% buyback and export to the United States of America. I was very successful in getting the clearances for foreign collaboration agreement and establishment of a hundred percent EOU. The unit was successful. The collaboration was for a specific period of 10 years; after that the technology was not allowed to be used in India. The collaborators did not extend the period.. The company was set up by Sri Alluri Venkateshwara Rao, in the name of Srinivasa Cystine private limited. The promoters were happy with my work and I had the satisfaction of getting the clearances in record time by doing the paperwork completely.

Proman Consultants Pvt ltd

With the advancement of time, the development of Pradhan stunted and Sri Dhananjay wanted to quit the company for some personal reasons and also because his industry needed more attention. After a while, I started another company by the name Proman Consultants Private Limited, with the same purpose of rendering consultancy and financial services. We started giving our services from concept to commissioning on the financial side and getting clearances from various government agencies. We started identifying viable projects with demand and supply gaps and advising prospective entrepreneurs. I am proud to mention that many projects were from our stable and were first of their kind in the country.

Bi metal bearings

The first project I worked on was a bi metal bearings project. This was promoted by Shri Edpuganti Bala Veera Raghavaiah chairman of Vijay Spinning Mills Limited. The project was the idea of my cousin brother Dr Murali Atluru, a successful technical consultant in USA, founder director of Diversified Technologies Consultants (DTC) Connecticut USA. Dr Murali is the son-in-law of Shri Raghavaiah, vice-chairman of the local board of SBI and a director of APSFC and Hindustan Photo Films in Ooty. He was also a successful entrepreneur running the seventh largest spinning mill as a single unit at that time in India. He was a man with principles and a person to fight for a cause. He was knowledge hungry and a keen analyst. Kirloskar consultants from Pune were appointed as technical consultants. I rendered the services for the clearance of foreign collaboration, industrial licence, company incorporation and advised on Company Law matters along with Mr Krishnan, a company law consultant from Delhi.. Being the first to give such services in Hyderabad, it was a immensely satisfactory experience for me.

A company by the name of Detroit Aluminium and Brass (DAB) USA was a leading manufacturer of bimetal bearings in USA and agreed to transfer the technology. There was a delay in making the first instalment of the technology payment. The management of the company abroad had been changed and the new management was not willing to involve in transfer of technology and setting up a manufacturing unit in India. By this time all the clearances were received from various government sources. We had already approached the Industrial Development Bank of India (IDBI) which was the premier financial institution in the country. That was the first time I visited IDBI. Mr Jaya Raman Aiyar was the manager concerned for the project. (Later he became E.D of IDBI and M.D of Stock Holding Corporation of India Ltd.) After the collaborator's withdrawal, we had withdrawn our application from IDBI for finance. The new management of DAB withdrew the technology transfer because of another reason. They said that Mr Raunak Singh of Apollo Tyres is claiming for the same with a document, but the approvals from the government were with Vijay Bearings Limited.

One stop shop for Tubulars

In 1983, Sri Dhananjay introduced me to Sri Kamineni Suryanarayana (KS) who was interested in setting up an industry to utilise existing facilities that were idle in Moulali Industrial Estate in Hyderabad. I had suggested two industries; one of them was manufacturing elevators since, the construction industry was going to boom and there were only two brands at that time in the country with a demand-supply gap. Another industry was to manufacture brake linings for automobiles as the automobile industry was looking up with new vehicles and big companies like Maruti. He liked both the projects but was not satisfied as they were low-tech. He liked the way I approached the subject and the analysis with which I selected the two industries. Finally, he selected the manufacture of tubulars used in exploration, drilling, and production of crude both offshore and onshore.

I had drafted the model collaboration agreement concerning the technology transfer and equity participation along with marketing support to be discussed in the USA with Baker Hughes. He discussed with Bakers and they had accepted the terms and conditions of the agreement without any change. During the discussions with Bakers, a couple of times he had asked for certain clarifications on regulatory matters relating to foreign exchange control in India and I clarified. The draft agreement was accepted by the collaborator in Toto. After the agreement was signed, he rang up and conveyed it to me. I was extremely excited because it had been reviewed by their legal and commercial departments and no changes were suggested.

We floated a company in the name of Oil Country Tubular Limited (OCTL). Our journey with OCTL continued for nearly two decades. We approached IDBI for financing. At first, it was rejected by the concerned manager in project finance department, Shri AKT Chari. The project was not understood in the right perspective. We requested IDBI to rethink on their decision. The reason for rejection was a report of an Investment Research

Organisation Pein Webber of USA. We requested Shri VJB Andrews, the concerned DGM to give the Pein Webber report for comprehension. After reading the report overnight, I concluded that it was a report on marketability of the raw material called green pipes. Both raw material pipes and end finished pipes are loosely called as Oil Country Tubular Goods (OCTG) whose stocks were piling up with manufacturers in the USA, Mexico, Canada, and Venezuela. In fact, it was a plus point for our project which had to import those pipes and end finish them in India. Next day, we explained the concept to IDBI that the rejection was on a wrong footing. Then they started rethinking and the project appraisal was finally put on board for financing. This episode gives us a glimpse of how financial institutions can also make wrong decisions and appreciate their rethinking after our appeal. We should also appreciate Sri AKT Chary (later GM) for his concern involving the funds for projects, until he was fully convinced..

Registering the name of Oil Country Tubular Limited was another story. The Registrar of Companies at first level rejected saying the name is generic which cannot be given without a prefix. I explained that 'oil country' is the prefix and the product tubular is used in the country's present oil exploration effort. SRI V.S Raju Registrar of companies Andhra Pradesh, who was a product of Nagpur University knew my connections with Nagpur and had allowed the name though it can be interpreted also as a generic name.

OCTL was the first major public issue from Andhra Pradesh with an equity base of 39 crores in 1984 along with an equity participation of USA and Mexican companies. Strategies worked well. I requested Dr R. Rajagopalan (Dr RR) to be on the board, who was also on the board of Reliance Industries Limited which is a darling of investors. I was his partner earlier. Dr RR was the first doctorate in accounts from ICAI. He was a cost accountant and a chartered accountant. When he took voluntary retirement from the ministry of energy as additional secretary, he wanted to practice so he started Rajagopalan and Co Cas. I agreed to become his partner on his request for two years. He only used my name but had not helped in my career. Due to my association, he agreed to be on the board of OCTL. He had said, "Because you asked, I agreed. So far I accepted Dhirubhai's request only", which was true. He was only on the board of Reliance Industries Limited (RIL). When he accepted, I was not his partner.

We wanted Datamatics Corporation or Reliance share Registrar to act as Registrars of the issue. Unfortunately, Reliance informed that they were meant for in house registrars for Reliance And Datamatics informed that they were overloaded with the work. Eventually, KARVY and Company approached us for the assignment. Shri M Yugandhar and his partner, with whom I am acquainted, met me and KS. K.S relied on my advice and appointed them. That was the first biggest public issue handled by KARVY and it was just the beginning of their rise in the field. Today, they are number one in the country. Initially, KARVY (Now K Fin Technologies) was just a group of chartered accountants who had started a non-traditional service with simple software. The public issue was oversubscribed by about 20 times.

The story of OCTL goes on. The company had difficulties due to Forex fluctuations during the construction period which was originally planned when the US dollar rate was at 12 rupees, which had fluctuated up to 18 rupees. Resultantly, the cost of the project had also gone up. Financial institutions had wanted matching promoters' contribution for debt-equity ratio. I argued that the increase in cost of the project was notional since there was no increase in cost of our imports and we were borrowing only in foreign currency and will be repaid in foreign currency as the company was earning only in foreign currency. That's how we avoided additional fundraising in equity. Institutions were also convinced. IDBI evolved a formula given by Mr Nadkarni, the chairman for working out the cost of increase estimates including contingencies. The project cost was worked out on the basis of these norms taking inflation index on major components of the project. Even forex fluctuation was taken into consideration on the basis of average fluctuation of the previous five years. Mr Mohan Gurunath, the dealing officer for the project followed these norms sincerely. Later these were called Nadkarni norms. It was a good practice which I followed for the rest of my life for project cost working, and most of my projects did not have great cost overrun. They might have faced time overrun in which some factors are beyond the control of the promoters and the government organisations. The financial institutions and banks which have not followed the norms ran into cost overruns and getting overrun approval is always a herculean task.

The project was referred to an Ad hoc committee of experts drawn from various connected fields including steel, pipe making, ONGC, GAIL, Indian Oil Corporation etc. I had to defend our stand from questions raised by 14 experts. The meeting was chaired by the executive director of IDBI, Mr Paliya. I could explain along with Mr Kamineni Suryanarayana (KS) even the technical matters that are required for the financial clearance. It was a test for me. It was a good experience and I faced three more Ad hoc committee meetings for three different projects later. KS was happy. When there was an international conference in Paris on oil technology in1985, he wanted me to represent OCTL. It was a compliment to my knowledge and involvement. But I couldn't go due to other commitments.

After the commercial production started, the company attracted many other technology transfers for some of the components from reputed international companies in this field. It is because of the planning of KS in creating a world-class facility unique in Asia.

The products were approved all over the world in global tenders. There were many technologies involved in making a raw steel pipe into a tough tubular to withstand the pressure of drilling thousands of meters below the earth's crust facing different terrains and gases. The threaded pipe gets automatically welded with friction welding. In case there is any gap called holidaying in the welding, it will create disastrous fire in the oil well. The coating given to the tubulars is also a special technology.

KS is a metallurgist by qualification from Banaras Hindu University and had worked in Rourkela Steel Plant and was also trained for some time in Kaiser Steels in USA. He was a man with solid technical knowledge and great observation; a person who can take challenges and withstand any stress without exhibiting even a sign of it. He fits into the definition of *Sthita Pragnya* in Bhagavad Gita. He is a friend in need for many of his friends.

We continued our services as public issue advisors, providing services to rights issue, advised on a case filed against Tata Iron and Steel Company (TISCO) in Monopolies and Restrictive Trade Practices (MRTP) Commission and won. It was a great experience to face the MRTP commission. I did the entire back-office work for an arbitration case against collaborator Baker Hughes Tubular Services in International Chamber of Commerce in London and we won the case. Mr Philips, a senior attorney from London complimented me for the paperwork and met me specifically in his effort to appreciate when he came to India on a different occasion.

All the services were rendered with single effort and dedication. On one occasion, I wanted him to take a legal opinion. He said, 'I believe in your analysis and advise.' During those days, there were no specialists on certain corporate laws in Hyderabad.

The experience gained in achieving the tasks in OCTL was very special.

Medium Density Fibre Boards (MDF)

Consultancy services to OCTL gave good mileage to Proman Consultants. We started advising another project with Italian collaboration from Sunds Defibrators for manufacturing medium density fibre boards (MDF). This was an effort of Godavari Plywoods Private Limited which was an existing manufacturer of plywood boards.

MDF was not available in the Indian market. The new company Indian Farm Wood Products Limited is one of the six companies to get the licence to manufacture MDF including Mangalam Timber, a company of Birlas.

MDF is a superior product to existing particle board, plywood, and other boards used as a substitute for wood as building material. The superiority is in strength, machining capability, lamination and lacquering. The strength is better because the wood fibres are bonded with a special resin.

We were involved in all the meetings of the Italian collaborator Sunds Defibrator and drafted the technology transfer agreement, incorporation of the company, preparation of the project report, corporate advice and completed the entire paperwork for clearances from the Government of India and financial institutions. We also undertook the counselling before financial institutions. Senior general managers Sri Dubral, managers Suryanarayanan and Sri Lakshmi Narayanan were involved in financial appraisal from IDBI. Ranganathan represented Proman in the final meeting of financial institutions. We got all clearances with our effort in record time. Shri I B Rao, an experienced engineer and a product of Tata Robins Fraser (T R F) a Tata's group Company, worked directly under Sri Rusi Modi, was the technical director of Indian farm Wood Products Limited. At every step of the project clearance, his contribution was of great help for us. We worked together and later he became a director in Proman Consultants Private Limited on our request. Institutions gave in-principle clearance and a letter of intent even before Mangalam Timber boards. However, financial closure could not take place owing to a puerile dispute of the promoter with financial institutions in settling dues of the existing Plywood company. The dispute was related to rupees 10 lacs that resulted out of the difference in calculation of foreign exchange translation. Andhra Pradesh lost a beautiful project, Proman's labour was lost, the acquired land is idle even now on the National Highway like a monument.

This is an example of how stupidity coupled with a litigant attitude impacts the growth of a business house. Pennywise and pound foolish at very high proportions was practically witnessed by me.

Multi-Speciality Hospital

OCTL was getting on to its track and Shri KS was planning to set up a hospital for his son Dr Sashidhar. Dr Sashidhar is a postgraduate doctor in surgery with urology as his specialisation. He was thinking of setting up a super speciality hospital. I told him that super speciality hospital is not a viable option. There is scope to set up a hospital with many specialities with its own outpatient wing. I explained that in 1984, Parliament adopted a health policy in which private sector participation in health sector was invited. Government's budget allotment would be limited for primary health, family planning, public health and sanitary conditions, preventive medicine, health education and development of Unani and Homeopathy as alternative medicines. The city and adjoining areas need hospitals with better facilities since most of the nursing homes set up and run by husband and wife combination do not cater to many requirements. Both K S and Dr Sashi were convinced. They asked me to start the work.

We had appointed Andhra Pradesh Industrial and Technical Consultancy Organisation (APITCO) for a market study. Dr Reddi Shastri, a senior consultant and my friend acquainted us with his managing director, and I explained the concept and the need for a survey. APITCO was a subsidiary of IDBI and Andhra Pradesh Industrial Development Corporation (APIDC) at that time. We were the statutory auditors of APIDC. The market study was favourable. Proman prepared the project and a pre-feasibility report.

We prepared the application for financial institutions. We advised promoters to collect information on outpatient details of major hospitals for deciding on various specialties to be set up. Dr Sashidhar immediately worked on that. We analysed the details and worked on the cost-benefit analysis on various departments and the required investments on equipment and the resultant income for preparing the project report. Dr Sashi and I visited Jaslok Hospital and Hinduja Hospital in Bombay. We had a question-answer session with Dr Ramachandran, the director of Hinduja Hospital. I liked the fully automatic laundry facility there. The investment for that equipment was 8 crores in those days. We studied and understood hospital planning, especially the planning of sterile areas in Jaslok Hospital. I suggested that sports medicine which did not exist in the south at that time could be a speciality in the proposed hospital. We wanted to visit Sancheti Hospital in Pune for that purpose. There was a lot of groundwork done before taking certain decisions and the project report was prepared on that basis. Believe you me, it was not just a spreadsheet with some estimates.

Shri KS got plans from some American hospitals through Dr Jayaram Naidu of Houston but did not use any of them. KS, a man of taste, and practical wisdom, in his own way, planned a unique hospital taking into account hospital planning, material flow, patient flow, location of nurse stations, isolated areas etc. When a leading hospital consultant arrived to suggest air conditioning and medical gases planning, I had told him that our country has not reached a stage where corridors can be air-conditioned. KS understood my emotional statement. The building was planned and the areas for air conditioning were separated. The project saved a lot of investment in unproductive costs. A well-planned hospital came into existence. It was the result of a successful teamwork that included me and Dr Sashidhar. Although KS totally left the decision making to us, the final decision and discretion was always with him.

It took an entire day for me to convince the representative of IFCI, one of the institutions funding the project. IFCI was not accepting the concept of a multi-speciality hospital as they only had experience of funding super speciality hospitals. Finally, the project was referred by IDBI to an Ad hoc committee consisting of 14 experts, drawn from the entire country. The questions of the members of the committee were answered by me and Dr Sashidhar. It was a great ordeal to get the project finance sanctioned because the rivals have tried their level best to influence the funding institutions not to finance the project. Eventually, we won over them.

It was a great satisfaction for me that I was a part of creating a good health care institution and first multi-speciality hospital financed by All India financial institutions.

A multi-speciality hospital was set up at a strategic place; the gateway to the city. The area covered in about seven km radius from Osmania Hospitals with a large population was not catered to by any hospital at that time. That was the beginning of Kamineni Hospital at LB Nagar in Hyderabad.

Hospital at Guwahati

Dr S. Saharia, a nephrologist of repute and our tax client, requested me to conduct a feasibility study to set up a hospital project in Guwahati in Assam. I collected the required data and prepared a pre-feasibility report. Mr Saikiya, Chief Minister of Assam who happened to be his patient promised for allotment of land. I advised Dr Saharia not to depend on the government for land which will have unnecessary strings attached. The cost of land in a project was not much and we could look to a growing area to set up the hospital in Guwahati. I discussed the project with Sri VJB Andrews, the general manager of IDBI in charge of the North East region. Mr. Andrews welcomed the idea. The delay was primarily because of land allotment. Shri Saikiya passed away in Delhi due to a heart attack. The project never took off marking the end of the proposed Jupiter hospital at Gauhati. Dr Saharia is a doctor with commitment and is the first to introduce dialysis in South India in the seventies. He was awarded Padma Shri by the government of India in recognition of his services. Jupiter hospital is a classic example of why one should not depend on the government for land allotment.

My approach to deal with the government was the same even earlier. Once, an NRI Sri M Babu Rao, a top executive from IBM USA, with others approached me for advice on a project for computer chip-making in Hyderabad. They told me that they were approaching Shri NT Rama Rao, chief minister of Andhra Pradesh for the allotment of land. I advised them similarly and told them they can get any extent of land in Patancheru at cheaper cost.

Another healthcare project for a doctor was worked out. This was a mid-size hospital with 125 beds but without a cardiac division and Cath lab. The project was set up at a centrally located place near Maitrivanam in Hyderabad. It was named as Maitri Hospitals. When the project was doing well, it was sold out. Although the promoter was a doctor, he concentrated on other business prospects later.

Hotel to Hospital Conversion Project

One hospital project report was prepared to convert a hotel into a hospital in Malakpet in Hyderabad. The hotel was not running successfully, so it was taken over by a doctor to convert it into a hospital. It was a relatively new concept for financial institutions. I sold that concept. .Later, a Warangal project and a project for Bhaskara Palace hotels in Hyderabad also followed suit.

Long Liner Fishing Project

The long liner fishing project was another first-of-its-kind project in India. The fishing in nearshore operations with trawlers was in practice in India. They were funded by state level financial institutions. Long liners, purse seiners and mother ships were used in deep sea fishing. Shri Yadla Ratnagiri Rao from Chiluvuru, near Tenali, a citizen of USA approached Proman for advice on the preparation of project report, licensing, arrangement of funds etc. He was a first-generation entrepreneur from USA without any organisational setup in India. His nephew Mr Madala Anil Kumar, a young graduate without any experience was my intern for the project. He was hard working with tremendous zeal and enthusiasm who collected a lot of information under my guidance.

We prepared a detailed project report with relevant information about the availability of fish, the types of fish in the Arabian Sea and the Indian Ocean, detailing different methods of fishing used in deep sea fishing. We also collected the international market trends and prices of fish and their variations in Asia pacific region as per the reports published by "Info Fish" Kuala Lumpur, setup by FAO (United Nations Food and Agriculture Organisation). During those days, buying a vessel licensing was required. The Agriculture Ministry was authorised to issue licences for fishing vessels. We applied for the licence. The ministry called for an interview with the promoter. Shri Anil Kumar and I, carryinga proper mandate on behalf of the company, appeared before the licensing committee consisting of six joint secretaries and senior bureaucrats (all IAS) from 6 Ministries. The meeting was chaired by the secretary ministry of agriculture, Shri Ardha Nariswaran.

Since this was a new method of fishing on Indian shores, the committee asked many questions. The representative of the ministry of industries asked if the fish can be tinned and sold. I explained that, 'the fish that is caught is processed on board and individually quick frozen (IQF) fish'. The targeted market was the United States and Europe. Still, the members of the committee insisted why it was not possible. He did not understand the purpose of saying targeted market. I explained the eating habits in different continents. People prefer tinned food in certain countries whereas other countries prefer fresh marine food, and the rest prefer frozen food. I also told that tin as a metal was not produced in India; we have to import which is not feasible, especially when foreign exchange fluctuations were rampant. I further said reluctantly, if the government insists, we can do it as second phase after successful operations.

The committee asked us to wait outside after our deliberations. After their discussions, they called us inside and gave the good news that the licence was approved. Finally, the committee appreciated my explanations and the amount of information that was given with authentic statistics which helped them to take a decision. Shri Ardha Nariswaran asked me, ' What is your basic qualification?,' I said, 'I am a Chartered Accountant.' "It is amazing" he said. The compliment I received from him is unforgettable..

I always tell my students that a well-trained chartered accountant can be a multi-specialist also.

It was difficult to convince the financial institutions as the project was a relatively new activity. Fishing was never treated as an industry, so IDBI and IFCI who were financing industries were not willing to fund the project. Banks were not willing to take up this because it was not supported by term lending institutions. ICICI started a new subsidiary called Shipping Credit and Investment Corporation of India (SCICI) for funding shipping activity, which was the new institution setup for funding shipping projects. It agreed to finance the project since import of a vessel was involved. It was the first project for SCICI and so they had no formal documentation formats even. Proman helped in documentation; it was a great experience. The project was launched successfully in Karwar on the West Coast. The company Royce Marine Products Ltd had gone for public issue, but the response was not overwhelming. The company operated successfully for some time. The chief promoter never shifted to

India. The remote control of management from the USA did not allow the project to go by leaps and bounds. This is a classic case of failure due to remote control. That is why lenders and investors always insist that the chief promoter should be present personally to steer the company.

Female condom project

This is another first of its kind product, a female condom. Dr Alla Venkata Krishna Reddy, a trauma surgeon from Wyoming in USA developed a female condom which is a new concept in the world. Doctor Reddy was the inventor of the product whose purpose was to elevate men's pleasure during sex. The condom is designed in the shape of a bikini worn by the females and the erect male penis pushes the pouch inside the vagina. The male reproductive organ does not differentiate the presence of the pouch of the female condom once it is inside. As a concept, this was welcomed not only in the US, but also by the United Nations and the World Health Organisation which supported this as a device for AIDS control. It can also be used by the gay community by reversing it. Mr Bob Sample, latex scientist from Akron Rubber was associated with developing the product along with the inventor and designed the necessary moulds. Dr Reddy spent a considerable amount of money on patenting the product in the USA. The product got US FDA (Food and Drug Administration) approval which is generally tough to get. The doctor started producing the product in the USA after patenting but the latex was mostly available in India and Southeast Asia, at competitive prices, which inspired him for setting up the unit in India.

We approached the IDBI for funding. The appraisal was taken up by the technology department since this was a new product and new technology. Mr Subramanyam, the DGM of technology department took up the appraisal. As a financial institution, IDBI was conservative and was aided by a similar team. It was a difficult task to explain the product, the concept, the process, acceptability due to habits of people and ultimately marketability. An attitudinal study was conducted by distributing the product samples to couples, social organisations, women organisations in India for involving in the study. Results were satisfactory. Ultimately this was referred to an Ad Hoc committee for approval consisting of experts from various fields like Rubber Industry, the competitors, the London rubber company, which is making male condoms, social scientists, gynaecologists etc. Doctor Reddy, Mr Bob Sample, Mr. Ranganathan, and I, attended the ad hoc committee meeting. The meeting was chaired by Sri Gopalan, the technical advisor to IDBI. On behalf of ICICI, a Deputy General Manager (DGM) at the time, Mr KV Kamath (later became chairman of ICICI) attended the meeting. ICICI expressed their unwillingness to fund the project. Mr Gopalan, the Executive Director of IDBI agreed to fund and deliberated that a project like this should be supported by technology department of IDBI and they will go alone. The project was cleared by the committee and it was funded by IDBI solely.

The project was set up in Gujarat, for the purpose of total export to the USA. However, Dr Reddy committed a mistake of selecting Mr Sanjay Munshi, an unsuccessful latex gloves project promoter, as his partner to implement the project since there was an existing setup and only part of the equipment was to be changed to produce the product. That is where he tried to save his investment. The partner lacked managerial skills and the project was a failure even in the initial stages.

Many prominent people approached him for partnership, since the product was approved by US FDA and a foreign exchange earner. Dr Reddy refused the partnership. Dr Manmohan Singh, then finance minister banned total imports and made it a precondition to earn foreign exchange for any imports which is why many industrialists approached for joint venture. Refusing the proposals was a wrong decision. Since he did not make up his mind to shift to India, he needed an experienced partner. Afterwards, net foreign exchange earning position improved in the country. India lost a great opportunity to make the innovative product.

Later Dr Reddy developed a male condom with little change in the design to give more pleasure for males since it is always felt that condom does not give full pleasure. The project was set up in South East Asia.

Dr Reddy's efforts in this research and his success and failure were discussed in New York Times in its issue on 11th April 1999, as a story and described him as Leonardo of condoms.

After some years Dr Reddy wanted to setup a radial tyres project. The tyres were meant for heavy-duty vehicles like buses and trucks. However, the consumption in India for radial tyres was not much.

Technical reports were made in USA with the help of Akron Rubber. He wanted me to prepare a viability report. He held discussions with Tamil Nadu government. Srimati Jayalalitha, the chief minister, wanted the project to be set up in her constituency.

It was not a bad proposal since it was very close to latex rich Kerala state. I suggested that transport corporations of Tamil Nadu participate in share capital with buyback arrangement of 50% of the production since these are meant for buses and trucks. Be that as it may, the discussions were not rendered very fruitful. The project never took off. The technical reports remained with me. Later Dr Reddy came and met me in New York on one of my trips to the USA. It was a courtesy call but we were recollecting our efforts for various projects.

Ever smiling Dr Reddy, was always looking fresh with a clean-shaven face and very friendly. He was restless, as his mind always wondered on innovating something new..

Dr Reddy, after a hiatus, came with another project idea of making cars work on hydrogen from water. I discussed his ideas and he even hired a sick unit in Hyderabad for his experiments. After some time, Dr Reddy went to the USA, where he was unable to pursue the project in full swing. He fell sick and passed away in New York a couple of years back.

Dr Reddy is a fine example of the one who takes research to the level of prototype product but not to commercial production. Facing all the hurdles from competitors and regulators with a broad chest, he was an innovator and an adventurous person.

Granites the new building material

Polished granite slabs were new building material in the 80s in India. Though slabs and tiles were in use, they were not so popular as marble since the finished product was not abundantly available in the country. Granite blocks were being exported to other countries. There were not many industrial units for cutting and polishing the blocks and slabs, with modern gangsaws. Deccan Granites Limited, an existing company involved in making granite slabs wanted to expand their operations by increasing the capacity and go to public issue. Mr Uttam Kumar, the managing director approached me for our services.

I made a presentation before IDBI. IDBI was reluctant to finance the project because a project financed by them in Chittoor district in Andhra Pradesh was not successful. I met Sri Gangaram, the general manager project finance and explained that the earlier project was working on wire saws, the technology was old and the production of polished slabs was of poor quality. The proposed project is working on imported gangsaws and it is an expansion of an existing, exporting, successful company funded by the state-level institution APIDC. Sri Gangaram said that they were conducting a study on the industry. I requested him to make the company as a part of the study since it is an existing operating company funded by state-level institution APIDC. He agreed. At that time only 10 gangsaws were working in the country of which two were with Deccan Granites Ltd.

We provided statistics on production, consumables, wastage, selection of raw blocks, their sizes etc for the purpose of study which were part of our detailed project report. We made the benchmark study successful and could fix the benchmarks for the industry. Mr Rajadan (general manager and later M.D of stock holding corporation of India ltd) and Mrs Godbole were associated with the benchmark study. It helped IDBI for evaluation of further projects in the granite industry and contradict claims of machinery suppliers and the promoters. The production of slabs and tiles is higher in Italy and other countries because the size of the blocks was large and gangsaw fully utilised all the blades to cut and there was less idle capacity. India did not have such mining operations, roads, bridges, culverts, and transport vehicles, and material handling equipment in those days. The benchmarks were fixed according to Indian conditions. Later there was an improvement in mining operations and modern equipment was installed in mines and the situation was improved.

The project finance was sanctioned; the company went to public issue and was very successful. Young officers in IDBI used to call me Dada Saheb by then because I had steered many projects with financial planning. The group of young marine engineers who started the project was also happy.

Afterwards, they requested me for my suggestion on any other project since Proman was identifying viable projects. I suggested pesticides and a couple of other things. I was requested to conduct a pre-feasibility study on pesticides which I did and submitted a report. However, it did not arrive at a logical conclusion.

With the success of Deccan Granites Limited Photophone Industries Limited, a company dealing with photographic goods, projectors, other studio equipment, and cinematographic equipment approached, for advice on the granite industry. Mr Abdullah Fazal Bhoy, the director of the company met me in Bombay in Taj President in my room for discussing on the industry. My friend, Sri B Ramesh, arranged this meeting. Mr Ramesh is also a reputed technical consultant who became a director in Proman. I asked for the present business details which they forwarded. They had large foreign exchange requirements for importing equipment. The restrictions on Forex at that time made them reconsider earning foreign exchange by way of exporting granite. I conducted the feasibility study and advised them to limit themselves for raw block exports which they can easily procure orders with their international business connections and procure the blocks in India. Specifically, I advised not to start industry along with mining which is mud and slush business, which may not suit the corporate culture of the company. They discussed our report in the board and the board conveyed their thanks for the advice and paid the fee. Within six months, the forex position eased and normal imports were allowed. Meanwhile, Tatas and Bombay Dyeing had also started thinking of venturing into granite, a low-tech line of activity to earn foreign exchange.

La-Mansion Granites

Another new entrepreneur, Shri P Janardhan Reddy from Warangal approached me for advice on a granite project. Warangal area is known for certain granite quarries like jet black, bronze-brown etc. Mr Janardhan Reddy was having lease rights and ownership for such quarries. He wanted to leverage them. We were fully involved in giving a total range of financial services for the project, including advice for initial public offer. This was also a successful project. Later, however, it ran into trouble. Mr Janardhan Reddy, an advocate by profession, was successful in the cooperative sector and was the youngest president of Cooperative Central Bank Warangal in the entire state of Andhra Pradesh. He was a decent person, a connoisseur of food and drinks. He was also one of the three general secretaries of the youth Congress at the National level along with Sri Ramakrishna Bajaj. We became friends. The evening discussion after a drink always used to be on politics of India in the post- independence era.

First two Computer companies

One of the upcoming fields in India in the 80s was computer hardware and software. Dr T Raja Rao, first doctorate in computer science from IIT Madras approached me to prepare a techno-economic viability report on his proposed project. The project was to develop certain software using Artificial Intelligence which was a developing subject at that time. He established Computer Vision Laboratories Private Limited for which we rendered the services for including the preparation of project report, project funding and auditing for a number of years. Dr Raja Rao is an outspoken person with simple clarity and good command on his subject with an interest in music.

Similarly, Sri V K Prem Chand, a computer scientist working in ECIL and a member of the automation sub-committee of the 7th Planning Commission to develop the computer industry in India, approached me for preparing a techno-economic viability study on his proposed computer software project. He established Frontier information Technologies Limited. Proman has done loan syndication for the project.. An extremely well-read and soft-spoken person, Prem Chand's good conversational skills enhance his gentle manners. He is also very much interested in Telugu literature.

These were the first two projects in the computer industry that were started by resident Indians after Sri Raj Reddy's OMC Computers Ltd. in Hyderabad. State Bank of India conducted a study for understanding the working capital requirements for the computer industry and tried to fix the benchmarks. This was a new line of activity without raw materials, production, inventories etc.

which normally determines the working capital. SBI selected three companies for the purpose of this study. Our two companies were selected out of the three. I was involved in discussions with SBI, along with the special group constituted on behalf of these companies. A report was prepared by SBI after the study, which was later adopted by RBI as an industry norm for providing working capital at that time. Proman contributed substantially for this study.

Frontier information Technologies Limited went for public issue with Proman as issue advisors and Proman certified the prospectus as a category 4 merchant banker. Dr Raja Rao's computer Vision Labs remained as a closely held company. Despite both the companies had teething troubles, they achieved certain milestones in the computer industry. Both these entrepreneurs became my friends and are in touch with me even today.

VLSI Project

Dr M Sanjeev Rao, chairman of Electronics Commission and minister in the central government also proposed a project for making VLSI (very large-scale integrated circuits) in Hyderabad. He discussed the project with K Keshava Rao (K.K) who was the cabinet minister in the Andhra Pradesh government. Keshav Rao asked me to do some groundwork on the project. I made a brief note and the same was corrected and improved by K.K. The proposal was sent to the Electronics Commission and the concerned department in the Ministry. I was proposed as the first director for the company. Unfortunately, Dr Sanjeev Rao met with an accident in Punjab and went into coma. We could not proceed further in the project and it was a no-starter.

Dairy industry in Private sector

In 1992, one day, Sri N Chandrababu Naidu (CBN) rang me up and told me that he was planning to start an enterprise in the field of dairy and dairy products. He sought our advice and financial services. I went and met him in a newly opened small office in Dwarakapuri colony in Hyderabad. We discussed plans and also his idea of pursuing cheese making. I dissuaded him to opt for cheese since its working capital cycle is long. As a new entrepreneur who is also a politician, it was difficult to get finance for working capital from banks. It was the beginning of the new era of liberalization and to face competition from foreign brands for cheese was difficult as a new company. Last but not the least, the quality of milk in India is not suitable for cheese making. He got convinced. A project report was already prepared by a Mumbai consultant. I requested him to give me a day for reviewing the details. He gave the report and I reworked and advised him to opt for liquid milk with powder plant as it will be an ideal start. Liquid milk can be sold on a daily basis and excess milk collected during the flush season can be converted into milk powder and the same can be used for making milk again during the offseason. He agreed and we made a fresh report. The dairy industry was earlier reserved for the co-operative sector. Later it got de-reserved where the private sector was also allowed. This was the first project in the private sector in South India.

We approached the financial institutions for funding. We went to SCICI (Shipping Credit and Investment Corporation of India), a subsidiary of ICICI and met Mr Singhal, the managing director of the corporation with whom I had associated with for the funding of long liner fishing project. CBN and I also went to meet Mr Patil, E. D of IDBI. He discussed the project with us and directed us to meet GM project Finance Mr Subramanyam. It was an easy approach for me since we had worked on a project with him on female condoms. Both IDBI and SCICI agreed in principle to support the project and communicated the same. After a month's time, we received a letter saying they were not supporting dairy as an industry. We understood the political foul play. By this time promoter's capital was brought in, land was acquired, advances were paid for plant and machinery and the construction of the factory was in progress. I advised CBN to go ahead in implementing the project with one chilling centre at Chittoor. Chittoor unit commenced commercial operations, milk sales were taking place in Madras and Bangalore and we had extended the financial year, earned profits and declared dividend. My strategy was to go for public issue as an existing profit-making dividend paying company. The company did not take any finance from any institution, the project was appraised by Bank of Baroda and for the purpose of public issue, and the financials were certified by the bank. We approached public for subscription of capital.

CBN asked me whether the public issue will be over by January, since he was going to polls after that. I said, 'Yes, that's how it is planned.' Prudential Capital Markets, the biggest merchant banker in the country handled the issue. Proman was associated with Prudential in two more issues. Mr Vaikunthanathan, who was in charge of Hyderabad office of Prudential and his team worked closely with Proman. The prospectus was prepared in

Proman's office. The issue was an overwhelming success and was oversubscribed by 54 times. CBN was happier about the success of public issue than his election results after a couple of months. That was the beginning of the success story of the company which is now popularly known as, Heritage Foods Limited.. We are associated with the company as their statutory auditors for 25 years in the best of the times and worst of the times. CBN came to power in the state. The financial institutions and banks who refused to finance the project asked him for favours.

He became a developmental chief minister and a role model for chief ministers of other states. Heritage became the number one dairy company in the private sector in South India with good product range. It continues its operations in Maharashtra, Punjab, and the entire south India in a span of 25 years, under the leadership of Srimati N Bhuvaneswari with the support of Dr V Nagaraja naidu, and later by Sri M Sambasiva rao, and Mr Lokesh and Srimati Nara Brahmani, an academically brilliant person with business acumen.

Heritage diversified into retail outlets for groceries, fruits and vegetables in three cities; Madras, Bangalore, and Hyderabad. This line of activity was running in losses even though it brought market identity and brand image for Heritage. Finally retail business division was sold to "Futures" group. Later, the company also diversified into the animal feed business, which I suggested as ancillary line of business in the first year itself for which land was acquired separately. Similarly, I also suggested manufacturing of packing material as another line of activity since the packing materials are purchased by the company in bulk and there is good prospect even as product independently. The study was conducted by Proman but it was not implemented. Had CBN not come to power he would have been a great entrepreneur. The loss to Heritage is a gain to Andhra Pradesh and Hyderabad which he developed with his vision. CBN is a disciplined, hardworking, shrewd person; a man who is interested in details and who takes time in making decisions.

Jelly filled cables

Communication industry was the thrust area for the government of India. The project on jelly filled cables was proposed by Mr G R Reddy, former chief executive of Hindustan Cables Limited. He approached Proman for the total range of financial services. We selected S.B Billi Moriya Consultants for conducting the market study. After establishing the demand for the product, we prepared a techno-economic viability report. It was easier to make the report since the chief promoter was a domain expert. We approached the financial institutions for support. IDBI was the lead institution and Sri A K T Chari was the general manager concerned for the project. Shri Chari made certain changes and suggestions to the project which we duly incorporated. After successful loan syndication, the company went for public issue for which we were the advisors. Prudential capital markets rendered the merchant banking services. The issue was very successful as it was oversubscribed by about 40 times.

GR Cables Limited was the last public issue (1993) Proman associated with. Later the markets fell and took a long time to recoup. Afterwards IPO became a different ballgame.

Project Advice to Sri Y S Rajasekhar Reddy (YSR)

After the success of Heritage foods, Sri Y S Rajasekhara Reddy (YSR), a member of parliament at that time called me from Delhi, to have a meeting with him. We were already statutory auditors of his company, Y S Properties Private Limited in Bangalore which was implementing construction works in Games Village. He wanted Proman to advice on a large farm which he wanted to convert it into an income earning enterprise. I have got all the details including the climatic conditions in the area, water table, it's proximity to urban markets etc. Ranganathan and I attended the meeting from Proman which was arranged by Sri Rajasekhar Reddy at his house in road number two Banjara Hills, He introduced us to his close friend and associate, Dr KVP Ramachandra Rao , his brother Mr Vivekananda Reddy and Mr Jagan Mohan Reddy, his son.

Shri YSR explained the purpose of the meeting and his plans on the proposed enterprise. The farm was in Karnataka. We had about three meetings on Sundays whenever Sri YSR was coming to Hyderabad after a parliament session. We involved another senior consultant in animal husbandry. We proposed a plan suggesting farming with a combination of poultry and dairy in the first phase, piggery including meat and sausage making in the second phase, since sausages were not being made in South India at that time. We also discussed the possibility of horse breeding. Sri YSR was very cordial and friendly in all the meetings.. After discussing the presentations internally, the groups agreed with the proposal and asked us to work it out.

After a month or so, there was one more meeting for setting up a cement plant. I suggested an existing running plant which was for sale. Upon request, we provided the details and also gave a Corporate Action Plan for the new project. Proman suggested working with a reputed cement consultant on the cement plant. Meanwhile, Sri Jagan Mohan Reddy's wedding took place (1996) in Pulivendula. As a well-behaved young man , Mr Jagan Mohan Reddy (presently chief minister of AP), personally came to our office to deliver the invitation card and extend the invitation on behalf of himself and his father Shri YSR. Later the state went to polls. Sri YSR became active in state politics as the leader of the opposition party. The farm project which was discussed, however, did not become a reality. A cement plant was set up by the group by the name of Bharathi Cements.

Medical College

Sri Kamineni Suryanarayana and Dr K Shashidhar proposed to set up a medical college in Nalgonda district on the National Highway where his industries were located. Application for setting up the medical college and the project report for the purpose was prepared by Proman Consultants. The report was very elaborate and I was told that Dr Kakarla Subbarao, a doyen in the healthcare sector and a member of Medical Council of India commended saying that this was the best report he had ever seen on a proposed medical college. I was really happy to hear the compliment. Dr P L Sanjeev Reddy sent a word to KS to have a look at the report. Another group also approached Proman for similar services for a college in Rajahmundry that we did not take up. KS set up a first-class medical college and it was the most preferred college for students and parents. The seats are given on merit even in management quota. I am happy to have associated in setting up a good institution which produces some of the best medical professionals in the country.

Author addressing the delegates at Shanghai in an International Conference of Accounting firms.

Author signing the balance sheet of Vijaya Bank. Seated next to him is Sri. S. Srinivas Rao FCA. Standing left is Sri. A S Rajeev present Chairman of Bank of Maharashtra.

Life in Profession-Independence and Value Addition

"Going through a cycle in the profession and witnessing the dilution of principles and practices is one dimension whereas standardising accounting and auditing practices is another dimension. I've been living in an era of gradual deterioration of integrity in expressing an honest opinion. Over four decades keeping up the independence has been a challenge."

Public Sector Undertakings

While pursuing consultancy assignments, the traditional tax and audit works were continued. Public sector undertakings (PSU) and Public sector banks(PSB) were also added to our profile. One of the major PSU works included Praga Tools Limited, a government of India undertaking. This was originally started by Nizam's government with Czechoslovakian technology to manufacture engineering equipment. Perhaps this was the first machine tool industry in the country. Their 'drill chucks' was a sought-after equipment among the products they manufactured. The company was having export markets also. Presently the company is closed down.

During the course of the audit, I did not accept certain presentations in the balance sheet and certain items remained unreconciled. The joint auditor along with me also accepted my contention. The managing director, Brigadier Abraham was not happy with our strong stance and we were ready to qualify. But I admired his tenacity in trying to convince us. He was mentally prepared for qualification on the accounts, and took out a small piece of paper from his table in which he drafted the qualificatory note with positive wording without changing the substance. This was how the independence of auditors was maintained. Central public sector undertakings were upright in maintaining their accounts and avoided adverse comments as far as possible.

Andhra Pradesh paper mills at Rajahmundry were big and were the earliest paper mill set up in Andhra Pradesh. It was a good audit with perfect maintenance of accounts by Shri A.L Maheshwari, head of accounts and finance, though a matriculate, was abreast with the latest developments in direct and indirect taxes, company law etc. The fixed assets accounting and the maintenance of the register were very good. We advised many companies later to follow such accounting. One year there was inadequate profit to declare dividends and the existing general reserve had to be touched for the purpose. In interpreting the formula for drawing out of reserves, there was a difference of opinion, between me and the management. The matter was referred to advocate Sri S. Parvata Rao (later justice AP High Court) for a legal opinion. Based on his opinion the dividend was calculated and paid out. This precedent helped us in deciding a similar situation in Vijay Spinning Mills Limited later. Sri P.J Mehta, a chartered accountant and finance manager of the company became a partner of our firm in 2001 and is continuing as senior partner.

APSFC is a premier state financial corporation in India which was originally started during Nizam's time. The example is followed by the government of India to set up such institutions in every state. A separate statute was passed by every state government to incorporate a state financial corporation. We were appointed as auditors of the corporation and there was an interim audit and final audit of the corporation with all its branches. During the finalization of annual accounts, I differed with management's view on certain practices and presentation of accounts. I held my ground which was disliked by the managing director, Mr Valliappan IAS. He thought a CA will accept whatever APSFC says since that is the breeding ground for clients in the case of chartered accountants. My stand was contrary to his expectation. I was only 27 years of age when I signed the balance sheet of that corporation, perhaps the youngest in the history of APSFC. Because of our strong stand, the next year's appointment was in the name of another firm as we did not yield under pressure. Normally the term of appointment is continuous for three years with yearly reappointment.

We never bothered about not getting the appointment or reappointment, but assuming that an auditor is expected to dance to the tunes of the managing director and general manager of APSFC was very unprofessional. It was a lesson for me also at a young age. However, I never accepted anything that was contrary to the accepted accounting principles and practices. The general manager was later raided and an enquiry was conducted for certain charges.

Later, we became statutory auditors of APIDC. Dr PL Sanjeev Reddy IAS was the managing director, later secretary department of company affairs in the central government. Dr Duvvuri Subba Rao IAS was the executive director of the corporation (later Governor of RBI). This was a good combination of bureaucrats and promoted number of industrial units in the state. It was a good experience. I suggested a cash budgeting system to ensure proper fund distribution for industrial promotion. After reading a book on efficiency audit, I suggested special monitoring of joint ventures by outside professionals, technical as well as financial professionals during the implementation of the project as well as a going concern. The corporation welcomed our suggestion and Dr PL was happy to introduce this as a special audit. The first such work given to our firm was to study AP Lightings Limited. Later a similar system was introduced by IDBI also and our firm was selected for a number of assignments. Now IBA is doing a similar exercise. I also suggested a register for investments and monitor the income from preference shares and debentures, which was also implemented.

It was a value addition exercise to the corporation by us as auditors. It gave a lot of professional satisfaction. Dr D. Subba Rao also nominated me as nominee director of API DC in NILE Limited and Rama Organics Private Limited. I received a letter from him when he was governor of RBI appreciating my book on Statutory Audit of Banks.

AP State Housing Corporation was another major corporation where we were appointed as first auditors. Sri N K Muralidhar Rao IAS, a senior bureaucrat who was earlier an income tax officer and also worked as a direct recruit officer in RBI quickly understood accounts and finance and was a good administrator. Initially, the corporation started building houses in cyclone-hit areas. Later, it spread its activity throughout the state. In the beginning, funds were distributed through district collectors and accounts were not properly maintained. I suggested certain controls, stock records and accounts manual for the purpose of accurate accounting, which was duly implemented.

Later Sri N K Muralidhar Rao IAS became the chairman of the state's Backward Class Commission. I suggested him to remove the word BC and replace it with IC; Identified Classes. I argued that the word BC casts a stigma on a certain section of people. What determines one's backwardness? Is it physical, mental or financial? Societal backwardness should be probed and identified. I gave him my article on this topic which was published in *Andhra Jyothi*. He agreed readily but forgot to give it as a recommendation, in his final report. When I inquired about it, he felt sorry. .

We eventually became friends. He used to visit our office even after our retirement as auditors of the corporation and his transfer from the corporation to some other post. I had the opportunity of interacting with Sri S.R Sankaran IAS, a selfless worker and a highly principled person. He was the chairman of the corporation for some time as secretary of social welfare. Later we became neighbours in Sapphire Complex in Panjagutta. I used to ask his views on our scholarship programs in BREAD. He was also the chairman of our interview panel for two years.

Singareni Collieries Company Limited is another feather in our cap. A coal company jointly owned by state and central governments and situated at the end of the central coalfields. It is a company originally started by the Britishers and later became a public sector undertaking. Mr Khwajah IAS, later Secretary of Government of India and the chairman of the administrative staff college of India, was very receptive to suggestions. Initially, he was a no man like a typical bureaucrat. We suggested improvements in fixed asset records specially land and other assets and insisted on its implementation, which were duly implemented. We also introduced corporate governance for the first time in the company. Ranganathan also trained the executives at the request of Mr Khwaja. Sri Kondiah Sastri, a good administrator and cost accountant, was heading finance and accounts who accepted our suggestions for improving overburden removal accounting. I was in the forefront and only used to be there for important meetings in the last year of our assignment, since I had administered a stent in my left artery in the heart. The audit was a good learning experience and a pleasant journey for Raju and Prasad. Many PSUs like Southern Power Distribution Company Limited, Central Warehousing Corporation, Rail Tel Corporation, LIC and our partners PJ Mehta, Balakrishna, and Dileep Kumar handled efficiently and whenever any issue of importance arose, I was always there.

The Board of Intermediate Education was another audit in which I discovered fraud of substantial amounts. I had given a confidential flash report to the secretary of the board explaining the modus operandi and the amount involved. Shrimati Vanajakshi IAS, the secretary of the board, was shocked and immediately suspended the concerned persons and enquiry took place. It actually happened in the earlier regime. Shrimati Vanajakshi was impressed with our findings. In a later posting as MD of AP MARKFED, our firm was appointed as statutory auditors. We unravelled fraud in Anantapur. Ranganathan went to Anantapur to establish the facts. In AP SSIDC, we were appointed as management auditors to enquire about the workings of various schemes of the corporation. After the study the marketing assistance scheme, quasi-equity scheme and equipment leasing schemes were discontinued. On the basis of our report certain changes were also made in the internal controls. Later, the Sheela Bhide committee recommended the closure of the corporation during Sri Chandrababu Naidu's regime. She was waiting to meet him at CM'S house when I was in a meeting with him. I told him not to close the corporation since 60 to 70 percent of the industrial production in India is from the SSI sector, in fact, we should increase the scope and enhance the investment limits of SSI. He said he will look into it but Sheela Bhide Committee recommendation were implemented to close the corporation . We were again appointed as auditors by the official liquidator to certify the accounts. Investment limits for SME were revised in 2020 by Modi's Government.

Central statutory Auditors of Banks

Starting in 1978 with branch audits of Andhra Bank, which was the first private sector bank, another private sector bank Corporation Bank was also added to our list of clients in 1979 as branch auditors. Meanwhile, we were also appointed as statutory branch auditors of the Indian Bank in 1979, which was a public sector bank. When banks were nationalised in the second spell, we lost both the private sector works. With our experience and the strength of the firm, we were allotted central statutory audit of Vijaya Bank from 2002- 2003 to 2005- 2006. During those days, audit term of public sector banks used to be for four years. Later, we became Central Statutory auditors of Andhra Bank from 2009-10 to 2011- 2012.After the cooling period, we were appointed as Central auditors of Allahabad Bank with its registered office at Calcutta for the year 2015 to 2018. We also acted as Central Statutory auditors of Deccan Grameena Bank, a regional rural bank appointed by NABARD. Sri S S Rao, our partner was of great help in central audits of these banks. After the division of the state of Andhra Pradesh, the State Cooperative Bank became Telangana State Cooperative Bank and we were appointed as the first statutory auditors of the bank. Although not directly connected with banking, we also acted as the auditors of IDRBT, a fully owned subsidiary of the Reserve Bank of India., an institution specialising in imparting technology and training for bankers in a computerised environment.

Handbook on Statutory Audit of Bank

With this experience, I attempted to write a book on statutory audit of banks with the title, *Hand Book on Statutory Audit of Bank*, specially dealing with commercial banks. The books available at that time were dealing with the theory of bank audit and a couple of books existing were discussing more about Branch Audit and less about Central Statutory audit. I felt that this gap can be bridged by a new book. The book was published in 2012. I followed a checklist approach as a practical guide for auditors as well as bankers. The book was released by Sri BA Prabhakar, the chairman of Andhra Bank and a chartered accountant, with his foreword and the function was presided over by Justice G Raghuram. It was reprinted in 2013 and an amended edition was published in 2017. The book was well received by auditors and many auditors told me that they were following the book at the time of audit which gives me immense pleasure. It received a good review in the IBA journal.

Author with Sri S Ranganathan FCA, Sri BA Prabhakar - Chairman Andhra Bank, Justice G. Raghuram and Sri J Venkateshwarlu – Central Council Member ICAI at his book releasing ceremony.

Author with Dr. V.K Saraswat – Member Niti Aayog, Sri P.S Ram Mohan Rao – Former Governor of Tamil Nadu and Dr N Bhaskar Rao - Chairman of Centre of Media Studies at his book releasing ceremony

LATER THINKING NOT LATERAL THINKING

"Early thinking in life evolves as time passes. In retrospect, it will only give mixed reactions. In traditional life, there is less scope for out-of-the box thinking or lateral thinking."

An independent mind-set accompanied by a CA qualification and reasonable affluence, encouraged me to try my luck in professional practice. My father never denied my proposal however my mother was not well due to angina and blood pressure. My aunts Kamala Devi and Indira Devi wanted me to get married, even though my parents were not so eager at that time. So I continued with my profession. It encouraged and satisfied my ego, if not my needs. My father supported me philosophically and financially. Finally, he asked me to make a decision on marriage. There were three proposals where he asked me to choose one of them. I thought they accepted the proposal in principle and wanted my nod. I selected one girl, Ramadevi whom I met formally in Secunderabad Club along with her parents. She looked like an Ayyangar girl. My parents wanted a girl from a family with at least two generations of education. Her mother Subhadra Devi's father Mr C Narasimham, a hard-working bureaucrat, was promoted to IAS in 1947. Father Kolli Ramachandra Rao Garu was a medical doctor working in state government service. She was pursuing a law degree at that time. It was an arranged marriage.. had never given a serious thought to marriage. In fact, I even asked my father once, 'Is marriage essential?". He answered my question by saying that human beings can identify their offspring unlike animals and derive pleasure in life from them. He was right and thatwas my later thinking. Our two sons Sai Thejasvee and Tapasvi, were the fruits of our marriage who later became software engineers with a well-educated background.. That was the order of the day and did their MS from Arizona State University and the University of Florida respectively.

Sai did his PhD from Arizona State University in computer science and his thesis was published by Lambert Academic Publishing with the title, *Quantifying the Trustworthiness of Social Media Content*. He worked as a postdoctoral fellow at the Massachusetts Institute of Technology (MIT). When I was writing this book, Tapasvi was appointed as the youngest vice president of Intuit Inc USA, an internationally reputed company. Sai became the director of datasciences in a group company of Livongo Inc., another international corporation. The academic achievements of children had their roots in Rama, who provided them an analytical approach to studies and even monitored their college studies.

Sai married Anusha, who completed her MS from Arizona State University. They have two daughters, Aranya and Amulya. Tapasvi is married to Sushruta who did her MS from Florida University. They also have two kids, Arnav and Kriti. I notice a lot of happiness in the eyes of Rama when she interacts with her grandchildren. They are the prerequisites of life for us in old age.

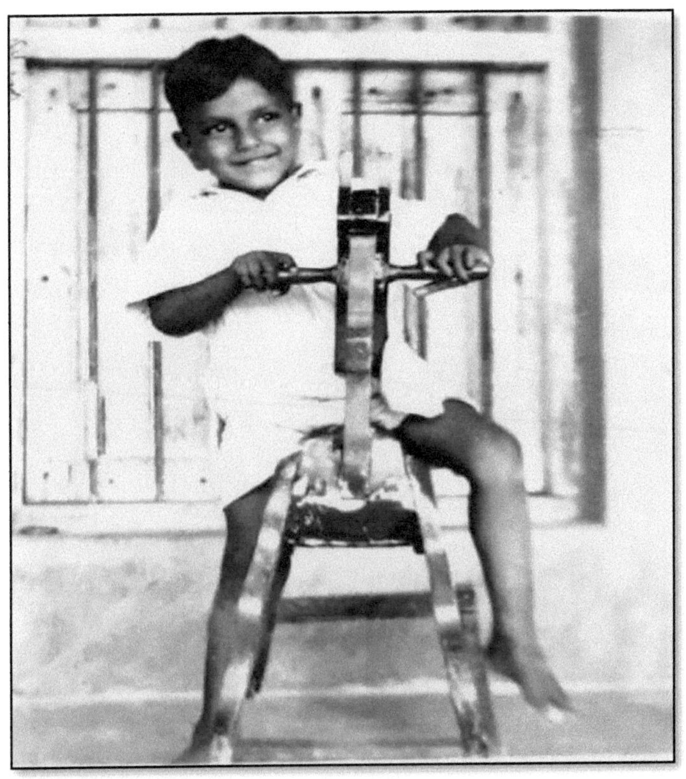

Author in his childhood

Author with his wife Rama Devi

Rama has a religious bent of mind unlike me. Though I am not an atheist, I think God is everywhere and is in everybody. It is difficult to explain, but I feel that humanism is more important, rituals and religious practices are not important according to me.. I notice a similar trend in the younger generation too. Some of the practices may be significant from a health and social security perspective. The rationale behind some practices was never even explained anyway. Nevertheless, I feel not harming others and helping the needy is our social responsibility and one can do so by seeing God in everybody. I remember the story of Surdas, the Sufi saint, where he was fainting without food and chanting in the name of God. Pitying him, a passer-by gives him bread, but a street dog eats it away. Surdas said, 'Swami, sorry I don't have ghee to offer you". That is the spirit of seeing God in everybody. Rama is always kind to people who are suffering from physical ailments and dutifully attends them.

I had some vague ideas about entering politics and wanted to contest in the 1983 elections from my constituency Repalle. I was sure of getting the ticket for contesting both from Congress as well as the newly born regional party, Telugu Desam. I studied the voting patterns of the previous elections in the constituency. When I revealed my intentions my father said, 'Knowing politics is not the same as playing politics', and added that the party system, as well as democracy, is deteriorating over decades. It is not meant for educated people. Once he disapproved, I did not dare to even think about it. I felt that there was no need for a village base, since my political aspirations will never be pursued anyway. Later, I understood his words as they turned into reality.

Later in life, I wanted to transform my hobbies like photography and singing into professional skills. Unfortunately, I was discouraged. I realised that making a living out of hobbies is tough as I can never lead the comfortable life I am accustomed to, from my childhood without much physical suffering. I concentrated on professional work. It was consuming a lot of time, which eventually led to the traces of hypertension at the age of 35..When I graduated in commerce, I wanted to pursue journalism. So I had applied to Bhavans College of Journalism in Mumbai. However, here I am, as a CA.

Be that as it may, I never stopped pursuing my writing skills. The first book that I wrote was on bank audits, titled as, Handbook on Statutory Audit of Bank. I have also been contributing articles for our monthly e-journal, Focal Point'. The articles largely focus on the latest policies or proposed legislations, industry, its history, origins, evolution in India, its problems and its analysis. So far, my articles have covered nearly 47 industries including those of the service sector.

I compiled them and published them as a book in two volumes with the title, *My Views and Reviews*. The first volume was released by Dr V K Saraswat, a member of NITI Aayog. The meeting was presided over by Sri PS Ram Mohan Rao, a former governor of Tamil Nadu and the book was introduced by my friend and chairman of the Centre for Media Studies, Dr N Bhaskar Rao. I am happy that many people use the book as a reference. Some of the articles were given due recognition by

Author with his son Sai Thejasvee and Anusha

Author with his son Tapasvi and Susrutha

SlideShare. *Bureaucracy Today* requested me to give permission to publish two of them in their monthly journal published from Delhi. ICAI requested me to write an article. My article on loan frauds and forensic audit was published in the official journal, *Chartered Accountant* in June 2019. Another article was also published previously by the journal *Chartered Accountant* on reporting requirements on FATCA and FBAR for Indian residents in the USA in September 2018. I wrote eight biographical sketches on domiciled Telugus who became famous internationally. These Telugu articles were published in *MISIMI*, a Telugu literary magazine. They were well acclaimed for the content as well as the style. This gave me a lot of encouragement to write in Telugu in future also.

One day I met a Maharashtrian astrologer in Sri Kamineni Suryanarayana's house. He introduced me to him. Without any previous knowledge about me, he said that I have two sons who are brilliant and will come up in life just by seeing my face. The second thing he told me was that I will build a beautiful house. I never took him seriously until the predictions came true. Both my sons proved themselves in their profession and came up on their own in the USA. I built a house on a very difficult site. It was my dream to build. I drew up the plans in a graph book to the scale and one of those plans was improved by the architect and ultimately the house came up well. Later I realised that the main floor plan shares some similarities to Kailasa rock cut Temple floor plan and the overall house elevation. resembles a palace in Basheer Bagh in Hyderabad. It is a coincidence. The basement is used as my library and activity area. I spend most of my time there reading, writing, enjoying music and singing with great peace of mind.

I realised in life that it is incorrect to think that I am doing something new or unique in life. Everything, every thought, every venture is temporary and time has an impact. Change is continuous. Changing in line with contemporary thinking and developments is essential in life without foregoing the basic principles.

POVERTY OF THE NATION

"Economic poverty subsists in a poor country when the results of development have not reached many people. The problem continues when the population is increasing in geometric proportions."

One day I was in the office of the Income Tax Commissioner. I was greeted by my old college classmate after exchanging pleasantries. When I was approaching the concerned officer, he said, ' Whenever your father comes to Hyderabad, please inform me. I will come and pay my respects to him.' I said, 'OK.' He told me that if it wouldn't have been for my father's help, he would not have completed his education and be qualified for this job. I said it is ok. In fact, I did not have a slightest clue about this. He belonged to a neighbouring village to Vellaturu. Later, when I went to my village and narrated this to my father, he told me that he never told this fact because his father incurred losses in his small-time business and requested me to help this boy. He said, 'I helped him eventually. I am happy that he is in a Central Government job. I never told you because he is your classmate. He may feel bad, and any help need not be given publicity. Then I understood the principle as well as his culture.'

In 1982, one gentleman came to take my advice and set up a partnership firm to undertake house building contracts from the state government and gave me his name, his father's name and Hyderabad address for drafting the deed. Immediately, I asked him, 'Are you from Kothuru Tadepalli village?' With a stunned look, he said, 'Yes'. Then I asked him, 'Don't you recognise me? I am Babu.' (That is my pet name) He sprang up from his seat and apologized that he did not recognise me. He left after his work was done and went back to my friend Sri DVR Murthy, a senior civil engineer who had advised him to come to me. He told Murthy Garu that when he was in a poor stage and unable to pursue his studies, my father had helped him financially to complete his education.. He was in a dilemma concerning the payment of the fees to Babu. In his next visit, Murthy Garu came with him where I told him not to worry about the payment and pay the normal fees as per our office norms. He developed his business and continued with our firm. When I was building my house, he offered me cement and sand but I said no. He said, 'I will repay my gratitude this way to my sir.' I did not accept, then, he said, 'Please pay me the cost at which I acquired the cement and I will send it in my own truck without transportation cost. I said OK. He sent a truckload of cement and sent the sand supplier and gave instructions to supply the best sand at market price.

Parents were helping the needy in my childhood, especially the educational needs. My father always used to tell me that if a person is educated, an entire generation is helped. There are a number of cases where he paid the fees in school where he was the headmaster so that the student's name is not removed from the rolls. I came to know about this in ZP High School Aruthegalapadu in Krishna district.

My mother used to buy the used books in good condition as total sets from good students in higher classes and used to give them freely to the poor students. She used to treat persons with scorpion bites with potassium permanganate crystals and lime juice and also used to give homeopathy medicine for minor ailments freely. I have seen this in Kothuru Tadepalli, an underdeveloped village where we stayed there for three years; from 1961 to 1964.

The village was only six miles away from Vijayawada. Imagine the plight of development in the country: the village was cut off from Vijayawada during the rainy season due to flash floods in Budameru. There was no proper road facility with causeways; there was no bus facility from either government or private operators. My father took up the cause and got a signature campaign done from nearly six to seven villages.. In the end, fair weather road and private services for buses was sanctioned. He used to tell me that every educated citizen has a responsibility to participate and contribute to the development of a poor country like ours.

One day we went to Vishnu temple in the village. My mother sent a word for the wife of the priest AcharyGaru. She did not come and some evasive reply came. After the *pooja* we went back home. The next day, the lady came and apologized saying, 'I have only one saree which I washed and got dried and I was wearing my husband's upper cloth, so I could not come out and see you, ma'am.' My mother understood the situation and immediately gave two new sarees which she had in store from her wooden cupboard. Then hearing this as a child of about twelve years of age, made me feel horrible about Indian poverty.

My father always used to quote Arnold Toynbee saying, 'American poverty is more horrible than Indian poverty but for me, I haven't seen American poverty, so I still feel Indian poverty is unbearable.' Disparity levels in India are growing wider.

Poverty in the middle class and socially known upper castes is more since they are slightly educated and due to the caste system, they cannot do certain menial works. This is the rural scenario. Rural poverty is worse because the opportunities for work are limited and one can never think of a white-collar job. The situation has not changed much. In 2014, I was getting a pesticide job done at my house in Jubilee Hills in Hyderabad. Among the boys who were doing the work, one boy seemed to be bright and understanding the work better. I observed him and asked what his education level was and he said he was MSc in statistics. I was ashamed to hear that he is working on a daily wage of probably rupees 300 and dealing with hazardous chemicals. From 1964 to 2014, 50 years passed but the story of poverty has not changed.

The stories of BREAD scholars were heart-rending. Dr Chitturi Ratnam of Chicago was toying with the idea of providing financial help for students going abroad who have completed their education in India. I came in touch with him because he is a good friend of Dr N Bhaskar Rao. I told him there are a number of brilliant students who are dropping out after intermediate with no financial help and not pursuing higher studies in spite of their brilliance so we should help them. Dr N Bhaskar Rao, the chairman of CMS supported my view. I was acting as alternate director for Dr Ratnam in Indotronix Limited for a couple of years. Sree Adusumilli Krishna Murthy Garu of Margadarsi Chit Funds was acting as alternate director for Sri M. Baburao of IBM. Dr NBR, Chitturi and I met a couple of times in Hyderabad and finally met in Krishna Oberoi (Taj Krishna now) to finalize the idea. The name was Bharat Research Education and Development. I suggested changing it to Basic Research

Education And Development. (BREAD) Dr. NBR immediately liked the word 'basic research' because he is a social scientist. Chittoori also accepted the name. North South Foundation was started by Dr Chitturi for the same purpose in the USA. Sri M Narasimhappa, a senior government officer from the income tax department and a common friend, was also present in our meeting in the hotel. We finalized the program. Ranganathan, our partner registered the society with Dr NBR as president, myself as vice president, Ranganathan as secretary and Vijay Babu, brother of Dr NBR, as a member. Later, I became the secretary and Ranganathan vice president.

North South Foundation started collecting funds to help this cause in Chicago from Non-Resident Indians. BREAD started its activities after receiving the permission from Ministry of Home Affairs to receive the funds from the USA. We started with a small budget of two to three lacs per annum giving 15 scholarships initially, which went up to 40 scholars per annum and for full course of four years, it was about 150 to 160 scholarships every year. Mainly encouraging professional studies of engineering, medicine and polytechnic courses, scholarship was meant for meeting the fees. Students were meritorious; we were only selecting candidates from the first 500 ranks in EAMCET common entrance test for engineering, medicine and in polytechnic courses, the first 100 ranks in MCA, from economically poorer sections.

The program soon gained popularity. Newspapers started giving free publicity and we were getting more applicants for scholarships. Seeing the poverty levels rejection became a problem. Even we started libraries to help the students in Osmania

University, Andhra University, and Sri Venkateshwara University Engineering colleges and kept the books under the control of the professors for the use of BREAD scholars. Buying professional books was very expensive. We got really meritorious students with utmost poverty level and illiterate parents. We were also paying for one side transport of both the parent and the candidate to enable them to attend the interview.

My office was the office for BREAD. Our staff was very enthusiastic to do the work related to BREAD. During those days, there were no cell phones and the entire paperwork was done by us. There was no internet for giving emails till 1997. Seeing our sincere work from Hyderabad, Non-Resident Indians from other states of Karnataka under the guidance of Shri Narayan Reddy, former vice-chancellor of Karnataka University and Bengal under the guidance of Sahana Majumdar, introduced the scholarship program. Later we expanded our activities in Gujarat, Assam and Orissa, though I was not happy with the quality of selection of candidates.

We also published an annual review on the lines of North South Foundation, suggested by Dr Chitturi. Dr NBR was coming annually for interviews from Delhi. One year, we invited his father, a freedom fighter and a teacher, to distribute scholarship cheques. Sri SR Sankaran, IAS and former chief secretary of Tripura, a sincere worker who had dedicated his life to the welfare of tribals was heading our interview panel for two years. Every year one media person was involved in our interview panel, Sri Varadachari from *Andhra Bhoomi*, on KK's initiative We also included Satish, who was famed for journalist's diary, Bandaru Srinivasa Rao, the director of *Doora Darshan* and Sri Krishna Rao director of AIR with Dr NBR's contacts.

After 10 years of successful operations of BREAD, it was proposed to honour eminent persons in certain fields who were not recognised and honoured by the government or other agencies. The jury for the awards was constituted with Dr. Karan Singh, Dr. Abid Hussain, Sri N Vittal and Dr. Ratnam Chitoori. We presented the awards in December 2000 to six role models.

After 12 years of continuous work, I stepped down as secretary due to personal reasons. It became my passion to work for these poor students due to my parental grooming and mainly when you hear their stories anyone would sympathise. When a boy from Srikakulam district got a seat in medicine, his father who was a fisherman literally cried when we gave the cheque and said he will be the first boy in my community to become a doctor. One boy from Vijayawada was selected whose mother used to stitch leaf platters (what we call *vistarlu* in Telugu) and make living out of the earnings. His father used to work as a server in marriages for serving food. The boy got a seat in engineering and after two years his sister got gold medal and got a seat in MSc mathematics. Our rule for one person in a family was relaxed for the girl. There are a number of such stories involving children of rickshaw pullers, agriculture labourers, construction workers and so on. Once we sent an interview letter to a boy in Nalgonda district, who got a seat in medicine. He came after one month with his illiterate father with one eye. I asked the person the reason for not coming on time. He said, 'In my village, the post is delivered only once a month. Still, I gave him a cheque and informed my committee.'

Imagine the conditions of our villages, the poverty of people and the lack of infrastructure even in a developed state like Andhra Pradesh and Telangana. What I have understood is developmental planning, with socio-economic dynamics is not enough and is not percolating down to remote areas even though opportunities are provided in the Indian Constitution. The takers are not coming forward because economic inequality and lack of money supports social inequality. Whenever I get into an Ola, I make it a point to ask the driver whether it is own or rented and what is his education level. Over 80% of the persons answered that they are employees and their education level is normally up to 10th or 12th Standard. My next question is, 'Why haven't you studied further?' In general, the answer is, 'My family conditions need support from my earnings so I discontinued'. Many of them are from urban areas, but some of them come from rural areas. With sympathy for those in need of help, I wanted to do a bit.

When I sold my ancestral house in the village, we contributed the entire proceeds to Moturu Ankineedu and Syamaladevi Trust for Education and Research (MASTER) by creating a corpus of Rs 30 lakhs, with the objective of helping the poor students for their educational needs. I am not fully satisfied with my work in the trust. Still, a lot of work is to be done in this direction.

In a recent report of 2019, Asian Development Bank revealed that the income level for an average Indian is 1.99 US dollars which is about 150 rupees per day, that is, approximately about 4500 rupees per month. In Indian conditions, a household comprises of at least four to five persons and they live on this monthly income. In case, more than one person is earning their livelihood, their living standards are better. Below poverty line is determined on two square meals a day without taking any other index or the basic needs like health, education and shelter.

As per the World Bank classification, India falls under the lower middle income group of 1026 dollars to 3099 US dollars per annum. The IMF estimates that 22% of the people earn less than $1.9 per day. As per UNDP, Oxford Poverty and Human Development Initiative, Multidimensional Poverty Index (MPI), the rate was reduced from 55 % in 2004-05 to 28% in 2015-16. According to ADB, the population with undernourishment is 14.5% in 2016-18. Death rate attributed to cardiovascular disease, cancer, diabetes, and chronic respiratory diseases, is 23.3% in 2016.

Statistical jugglery may refer to many things, Daridra Narayan introduced by Swami Vivekananda and popularised by Gandhiji as a concept is here to stay with shirtless and shelterless masses. From *Challenge of World Poverty* by Gunnar Myrdal in 1972 to *Poor Economics* by Abhijit Banerjee in 2011, both Nobel laureates for economics, things have not changed much, irrespective of many programs of the government. All this is because of population growth. Failure of not making family planning mandatory is proving that India is a rich country with poor people. To understand this reality Scotch whisky Communism is not necessary, only an understanding mind is required.

While completing this chapter, India is reeling under covid-19 and several months have passed which has impacted trade, industry, travel and resulted in unemployment, loss of income, in many spheres. Anyway, we have to forget growth dynamics since IMF itself is unable to assess the loss globally due to this pandemic. In a situation like this just imagine what would be the fate of daily wage earners, small vendors, artisans and the like in a country like India.

Author along with N Bhaskar Rao and Dr Ratnam Chitoori along with the members of jury of BREAD and Role model awardees at the role model awards.

Author inaugurating Vijaya Bank's counter at All India Technical and Industrial Exhibition in Lucknow

Friends, not Masters

"My studies shifted from Krishna to Guntur district and back to Krishna district. Out of my 70 years of life, 45 years I have spent at Hyderabad in profession and 25 years for my studies in Zilla Parishad schools, colleges in Guntur, and chartered accountancy in Madras. The friendships I made in student days were not significant and not continuous due to frequent shifts. A major part of my life I spent in profession and in Hyderabad and can mention some, long-lasting friendships I made."

Dr K Keshava Rao (KK)

Kancharla Keshava Rao, son of Niranjan Rao; that is how I remember drafting a deed for him in 1977 when he was selling his *Daily News*, a small newspaper to Mr Kandanati Chennareddy. Ten years senior to me, KK is ten times well-read and knowledgeable. I am impressed with his skills as a politician. His friendly nature sealed our friendship. This was probably the first friendship I had ever made in Hyderabad. Our conversation used to be more on current topics. After the sale of his newspaper, he used our office as his office for nearly nine months. Many politicians who became very prominent later in congress politics of AP were visiting our office to meet him. I was not married yet at that time and used to spend time together along with my partner MARK Raju. Both of them made me a member of the Fateh Maidan Club (FMC).

He was keen on producing movies and many stories were reviewed. Shri BS Narayana was selected as a director. Finally, a Malayalam novel was selected as a story for producing the movie, *Nimajjanam*, whose initial work was done in my office, on my table. KK, an Urdu medium student, was not very comfortable in reading and writing Telugu in those days. I was helping him in understanding the stories which were under consideration for the movie-making. I was involved in scriptwriting for *Nimajjanam*

He contested for Legislative Council from the graduates' constituency and the work of enrolling voters, preparation of voters list, planning the campaign was done from our office. He got elected and soon became vice-chairman of the Legislative Council. A student leader and secretary of Osmania University Students Union, a youth Congress leader, got trained and worked in "Link" and "Patriot" in Delhi with his bachelor's degree in journalism. He made a mark in the Legislative Council as chairman and became cabinet minister for small scale industries, labour, and education.

When he was the education minister, he wanted to introduce the education policy for the government of AP like industrial policy. He wanted me to help him in formulating the policy since he was not happy with the secretary of the ministry, an IAS officer. He kept at my disposal a plethora of books on education and a room in the house. I went through the relevant material and noted down the points and made a note mainly on Dr DC Kothari's report on education. He went through my note and we discussed it for approximately two to three nights. He typed the policy himself and he was proud that AP was the first state to introduce the policy.

He was the person who introduced the concept of open-university and started it in AP, which the government of India adopted later.

A stormy petrel in politics, bubbling always with zeal and enthusiasm worked with the chief ministers Dr M Chenna Reddy, Sri T Anjaiah, Sri Bhavanam Venkat Ram Reddy, and Shri K Vijaya Bhaskar Reddy. When there was a reallocation of portfolios, he asked me which portfolio to opt for. I told him the education portfolio since he represents the graduate constituency and is interested in that line. He said even CM Sri Anjaiah was suggesting the same. It was a coincidence that both when T Anjaiah and Venkat Ram Reddy were changed as chief ministers he asked me to accompany him in my car to go to their official residences; one was in Greenlands and the other was in Kundan Bagh.

When a devastating cyclone hit Andhra, Mrs Indira Gandhi visited the cyclone-hit areas without any government protocol and security. On that issue, six ministers resigned from the cabinet of Mr J Vengal Rao and assembled at his residence to give a press statement. He asked me to come immediately from my office which was in Tilak Road Abids. I drove and reached his house in about 20 minutes while the press persons and ministers were still in discussions. He said, 'I want you to go through the statement we are releasing.' That was the kind of relationship we maintained.

One day from Bangalore, he rang up and asked me where I was. I said I was in my office. He said that he wanted to talk to me. I understood, that he needs to take some decision. I took Ranganathan along with me to his house, by the time he reached home from the airport.

He told us that Chief Minister YSR was offering him two options, the post of Deputy Chief Minister or Rajya Sabha membership and, asked me for my opinion. Both are good positions. I told him "Deputy CM is not a post; it is only a cabinet ministership and you are not even an MLA". Further, the term of the government is halfway through. Given his education, intellect, political acumen and experience, I felt he would shine at the National level in Rajya Sabha. We discussed these factors and assessed. He was convinced. After a couple of drinks, we left. He conveyed to CM and accepted Rajya Sabha, served two terms, became the parliamentary party leader. For his nomination as a Rajya Sabha member third time, I was in Bombay. Covid was rampant there. On 6th March 2020, He conveyed the news of his nomination. The next day I returned. He asked me to come by and review the papers personally before he signs, and file the papers. He is in his third stint as MP.

He was always friendly and affectionate with a lot of confidence in me. He trusted in me as a friend, sought my counsel and had faith in my judgement. I respected his intellectual abilities and analytical skills. Our friendship spanned over four decades. Even though we meet less than we used to when we were young, the fondness and the mutual admiration remains.

IB Rao (IB)

Inaganti Bhujanga Rao, a mechanical engineer who worked in Tata Robins Fraser (TRF) and a blue-eyed boy of Rusi Modi, started his technical consultancy at Hyderabad after he retired. He is from Guntur district. When we were appointed as statutory auditors of Jubilee Hills Cooperative house building society by the registrar of co-operative societies Andhra Pradesh, he was the secretary and I continued for three years in that position and made suggestions to improve their systems and internal controls which were maintained in a crude way. As a shrewd person, he agreed and as a secretary implemented and started maintaining certain subsidiary registers and basic documents for books of prime entry. He liked my approach to audit as improvement-oriented and not a fault-finding mission.

In course of time, we came to know that we have many common friends and our friendship continued. He is 13 years senior to me, currently taking life easy in Texas USA with his son. He was the director of Proman Consultants Private Limited.

One day when we were discussing in general, I suggested that Jubilee Hills society requires a club and told that the members of the society are from all walks of life and many of them are seniors in their respective fields. It was a good mix of people to form a good club. Immediately, he said we created a community centre and the same can be used as the building. Let's start the work. I drafted the constitution and rules. It was typed in his office. We named the institution as Jubilee Hills International Centre. We even wanted to affiliate with some international centres like India International Centre. The task of convincing Sri AV Ranga Rao, the president of the society fell upon me. We selected the best governing council members as the first committee to represent all walks of life. I was the first treasurer and continued to be so for about six years. The council wanted me to continue but I was busy doing consultancy work which frequently demanded travelling out of Hyderabad and I felt I will not be doing justice to my job. So I requested them to relieve me when the term ended. I formulated the total rules, regulations, documentation, MIS, presentation of the balance sheet, and also, conducted elections.

It was a great time for the good friendships I made. One such friendship was with justice Koka Ramchandra Rao Garu, who was our President and was also the former Chief Justice of Andhra Pradesh High Court. He comes from an illustrious family of eminent jurists and was son in law of Justice P V Rajamannar, Chief Justice of Madras High Court. One day I was discussing two stories written by Justice Rajamannar "*Vankaya Koora*" and " *Sardar Papadu* ". He was amazed at my insight into rare literature in Telugu. He was a man of ready wit. I advised him on tax implications and tax planning of properties devolved on legal heirs of late Justice P V Rajamannar.

I B and I travelled in connection with consultancy works, handled by him for Medium Density Fibreboard "MDF" project and the Longliner Fishing project. I B is a friend to many people and kept in touch with every person right from his college days, who genuinely liked him back. He is a very easy going person and "no problem" is his usual dialogue. When I am writing this, he sent me an email that his granddaughter got engaged to Leonardo, a Brazilian doctor. He also developed Jubilee Hills Public School where I was associated with initially. A senior scientist from DRDO and president of the Jubilee Hills Cooperative House Building Society, Sri AV Ranga Rao wanted me to be on the committee of the school but I said no because I was too busy at that time handling many projects and public issue works. IB put all his personal efforts to build up the school from an ordinary two room tenement to an institution. Later, I was on the committee for a number of years as joint secretary for some time and then treasurer. Today it is one of the sought-after schools in Hyderabad.

Baddenahal Virupaksha Goud. (Goud)

The first time I met him as the executive director of APIDC was when we were statutory auditors. He was deputed from IDBI for a short period when he was a senior manager from IDBI, became its executive director in later years and became managing director of Stock Holding Corporation of India Ltd. He is very close to Sri K Vijaya Bhaskar Reddy's family. He was taking advice on his tax matters and became a friend. He is a person who is genuinely interested in the industrial development of AP state and was giving guidance to entrepreneurs of AP who were approaching IDBI as a financial institution. He was guiding them even though he was not in the Project Finance Group. Knowing our work in Project Finance and public issue strategies, he had suggested Proman's name to Dr A V K Reddy and we also advised him on the female condom project. Dr Reddy also understood that we are devoted professionals. Even in the case of GR cables Limited we were involved from concept to commissioning and our name was suggested to Sri GR Reddy by Sri Goud. He is a person with a good heart with a helpful nature. When he was the managing director of Stock Holding Corporation of India Limited, Sri L Viswanathan and Mr Basu spoke to me about introducing internal audit in their branches. I read an article on this topic in the official journal published by The Institute of Company Secretaries of India, taking some clues from that, requirements of NSDL, and the SEBI coupled with our internal audit exposure, and internal audit standards, drafted a program and sent to them. They accepted with appreciation and it was first implemented in Hyderabad and later it was adopted in other branches also. We served as internal auditors for five years at Hyderabad and modified and improved the program whenever required as per regulatory requirements.

Dr N Bhaskar Rao (NBR)

Nagulapalli Bhaskar Rao Garu, a social scientist and psephologist, was the one who popularised election studies, predictions and analysis of election results in a scientific manner in India right from the days of Mrs Indira Gandhi. He received his doctorate from Kansas University USA in 1960. 10 years older than me, we share our thoughts on many contemporary issues. The first time I met him was in the office of Godavari Plywoods Private Limited along with Dr Tella Subba rao a couple of times. I met him with Adiraju Venkateswara Rao later who was my client. We became friends because we shared many mutual friends . Whenever he was visiting Hyderabad, he was in touch with me and I used to meet him in Delhi. One day as a chance we happened to meet him in Nizam College grounds along with Adiraju for an election meeting of Rajiv Gandhi. My wife and her sister Aruna also attended the meeting along with me. I introduced them to Adiraju and NBR. It was a surprise to me that my wife comes from the same village of NBR and his father knew my father-in-law very well.

NBR is a good conversationalist and a friendly person. Our friendship continued for nearly four decades. I am his regular guest at least one evening in India International Centre Delhi for dinner all these years. He introduced me to many of his friends in Delhi. He was known as Delhi Bhaskar Rao in Hyderabad in those days. He introduced me to Khushwant Singh, the former editor of

Illustrated Weekly of India. I admire Kushwant Singh a lot for his journalistic skills. He was on the social audit panel of *Prasar Bharati* along with Justice Sawanth for which NBR was the convener. NBR invited me for an exclusive dinner with him in Hyderabad in Bhaskara Palace Hotel. (Presently the building is used for running a hospital.) It was an interesting evening. Again, Khushwant Singh invited both of us to his home, when I was in Delhi. It was a pleasure spending time with him.

He requested me to float a society for media studies in Hyderabad. I did it but it did not take off. While implementing the Heritage project we wanted a study to be conducted on the Milk products market in the south, especially in cities like Bangalore. His organisation did it and was useful for certain management decisions. Similarly, when CBN was preparing for elections in the last quarter of 1992 I suggested to make a poll study and suggested NBR's name to CBN. He knew him well. Immediately. I called from CBN's phone in Heritage and connected with NBR after briefing the purpose to him. They both talked to each other and NBR's organisation conducted the survey. He never charged for his services and conducted a similar study in Tamilnadu at the request of CBN keeping the prospects of DMK and Karunanidhi in view, for which he has not earned money but only the wrath of Jayalalitha. Vision 2020 report for Andhra Pradesh was also his brainchild. Before CBN came to power, a small booklet in my name reflecting the agenda of the new government was published by him.

In our discussions, NBR and I always talked about the growing poverty in the country, and the rural poor's inaccessibility for higher studies. Dr Ratnam Chitturi of Chicago, who is a good friend of NBR was also sharing similar concerns, expressed that a number of

NRIs want to help people from their village schools. I told him that up to 12th standard, education is affordable but later it turns expensive. Helping students from their own village as the base would be parochial and will not serve the purpose. NBR supported my view and that's how BREAD was started. When I stepped down after 12 years as secretary of BREAD, NBR who was also the president of BREAD, stepped down along with me and said either we go together or step down together. That is the straightforward attitude of NBR. He is a prolific writer and has published a good number of books. *Chronicles of a Village Boy in New Delhi* is an autobiographical sketch. Other books include a *Handbook of Poll Surveys in the Media, Unleashing the Power of News Channels, Citizen Activism in India and As we Sow so we Reap*. We interact regularly and think of the nation and the direction in which it is moving.

Kamineni Suryanarayana (KS)

The journey of our friendship started from the day of industrial licence application for setting up manufacturing facilities for the end finishing of tubulars used in the oil industry. Started as a client and became a well-wisher and friend. We travelled in India, the Middle East, and the USA in connection with his work. During a similar trip to Bombay, my father met with a freak accident near our flat in Amrutha estates in Hyderabad and was admitted to the hospital. My wife Rama informed him about this, keeping this as secret. He only said, 'We will return back to Hyderabad on the pretext that the meeting in Bombay was not going to take place and Indian Airlines was going on strike.' He did not talk about my father's accident till we reached Hyderabad. By that time my father went into a stage of coma, he started explaining to me while going to the hospital from the airport that it was a head injury but there is no sign of injury and there was an internal haemorrhage due to external impact. I told him this is a case cited in the novel, *Final Diagnosis* by Arthur Hailey. He was really surprised to see me cool and composed and with a strong mind. I told him that my father taught me attachment and detachment should be equal in life, which he too practiced. He was like a Rishi. My father passed away the next day early morning. He stood by my side and gave me moral support which I can never forget. Similarly, when I had to be administered a stent in the left artery of my heart, he reached the hospital early in the morning at 7 o'clock even before I was taken to the Cath lab. That was his concern for me. Although I rendered my services with total dedication to his companies, to find someone like him in the present time is rare. We continued our friendship for nearly four decades whether we were his auditors or not. He advised Sri Chandra Babu Naidu to take our advice and services when he was setting up Heritage foods. He also told me that I have to take care of everything that is required since Babu cannot devote much time. He is like a godfather and friend in need for many people.

Donthineni Seshagiri Rao (DSR)

One day when I was with Sri M. Dhananjaya, a handsome person, well-dressed in white safari walked in. Dhananjaya Garu introduced me. I left the place since they had an issue to discuss. A few months later he sought my advice on a certain issue. He wanted his company's assets to be valued which I took up. Later, I advised on introducing the costing system in his company. In a year's time, he wanted to change his existing auditors as he was not getting timely advice. The journey with him too continued for nearly four decades.

We had to take up arbitration between him and his partner Shri Kanneganti Papa Rao. I B also joined me in our arbitration team and after having a number of meetings we arrived at the formula and both of us went to meet him in an unconnected village where Sri Papa Rao was living, near Sindhanur in Karnataka surrounded by cotton fields. The journey to the village was a great task as the road was not fit for a car. After a certain distance, IB and I reached the place by a tractor. By the time we completed our task and returned, IB became sick due to cotton dust allergy. Somehow, we returned back to Hyderabad.

The Arbitration Award was acceptable for both. The matter was settled amicably. Sri Papa Rao, father-in-law of Sri Jayaprakash Narayan of Loksatta, was a very well-connected person, who had graduated in agriculture sciences. It was difficult to convince him but he is a well-informed gentleman. After the arbitration was over, Papa Rao Garu visited our office. I asked him, 'Sir, you know that I am chosen by Seshagiri Rao Garu, why you have not appointed your own arbitrator?' He said, "I enquired about you with a couple of people and SRI S Parvatha Rao advocate (later justice Andhra Pradesh high court) told that you will not get a more decent person than him, perhaps you should know that no university degree is equal to this certificate of Shri Parvatha Rao. I consult him on all my personal matters and value his words.' Sri Seshagiri Rao was also happy about the arbitration. We both were on the first committee of Jubilee Hills International Centre and later on the committee of Jubilee Hills Public School as secretary and treasurer where many critical decisions were made by us for the growth of the institutions

Tatineni Krishna Prasad (TKP)

Uni Ads is a well-known name in Hyderabad in Outdoor Media. TKP was its founder and also its chairman and MD. He was equally popular in many circles irrespective of party lines. He came in contact with me when there was a tax issue to be advised. His accountant and my student V Sivakumar discussed the issue to change the auditor. I said, 'I don't believe in anybody who wants to change the auditors when there is a problem. Let them continue, we can still advise and represent the case.' Later I discussed the issue with the company's auditor and told him, 'I would like to advise the company on this tax issue as a professional courtesy and as per professional ethics I am informing personally'. He was glad that I informed him personally. Later we became auditors of the company when the existing auditor shifted from profession to investment advisory services. We took up the case. Ranganathan successfully completed the case and got a refund of nearly a crore of rupees in those days. One great thing I found in Prasad was he wished that everyone should prosper. That's how he made most of the senior employees continue with him as partners in one business or the other. He was a magnanimous man. When we proposed a business for him in real estate in Banjara hills, he said that you are one of the partners and distributed the profit on its disposal. He used to like my second son Tapasvi and always wanted him to come back to India after his studies in the USA and start an enterprise. He used to visit me, have a cup of coffee and breakfast at my place whenever he wanted personal advice. His health deteriorated and the doctor never allowed him to move, still he visited me twice and wanted me in his hospital in Madras. He was an emotional person with a good heart, always outspoken. In his death, I lost a good friend.

Moments to Cherish

"Surprises in life give momentous happiness and they continue as reminiscences. Mentioning only a few such moments which are neither milestones nor turning points."

Darshan of Lord Sri Venkateswara

Nageswara Rao's (my roommate) family visited Tirupati for some religious purpose. His parents asked both of us to come from Madras. We both stayed in Bhimas hotel (1972), while his parents were staying with their relatives in Ganguntra Mandapam Street in Tirupati. Around lunchtime, we both went to see his parents. Sri Dattatreya, his father was a leading lawyer in Kadapa district. He proposed that he would like to pay a visit to Sri Ananthasayanam Iyengar on the same street and he took me along with him. Sri Ayyangar was known as a walking encyclopaedia when he was practicing in Madras High Court. He was a former speaker of Lok Sabha and retired as the governor of Bihar. Simple house, longish like a railway bogie, he was sitting in an ordinary easy chair in a small veranda. It reminded me of my father's meeting with Dr BC Roy in Calcutta along with Shri N G Ranga around 1932. My father used to tell me that Dr Roy stayed in a two-room tenement. From the first room, he used to see his patients and stayed in the same place even as chief minister of Bengal. What a simple living and high thinking. I am really surprised that Sri Ayyangar spoke on contemporary issues. Sri Dattatreya introduced me to him and when I told him that I belong to the family of Dr E Raghavendra Rao, he was very happy to know about it and talked to me affectionately.

After the visit, we climbed the hill. Nagesh's family contacted the Peshkar for darshan. By the time we went, the Peshkar was not available. He was on leave meanwhile a classmate of mine Mr Seshagiri, whom we used to affectionately call "Anna", was on the premises. His father was the health officer of TTD. He saw me and asked, 'Prasad, why are you here? Why did you not contact me?' I told the purpose. During those days, there was no break *darshan* I think. He came to the queue and stopped the flow and made our Darshan easy. Nagesh's family profusely thanked me. I felt it was a God-given opportunity.

A similar thing happened in 1984 when I took my family for the tonsure of my second son. My friend Mr M R V Prasad, the son of Sri M Dhananjay made arrangements for cottage and arranged a car for us. I was surprised that the chairman's car was waiting outside the railway station for us. Everything was easy, seeing the car with the chairman's board. The driver told that this car is only allotted for the VVIPs and the chairman was out of Tirupati. After entering the temple premises, they stopped the pilgrims because the deity was carried in a procession around the temple for *Vasanthotsavam*. Chief executive officer, Sri Kumaraswamy Reddi saw my father-in-law, Dr Ramachandra Rao Garu and signalled to join the procession along with him. I felt that God himself came to invite us into the temple. We witnessed the *Vasanthotsavam* where the procession finally ended.

Once I went to Shirdi along with Rama, Thejasvee and Tapasvi. *Darshan* was stopped by the time we arrived. We paid our respects to Baba from outside, went around Dhuni and other places in the temple premises.

Sri M Narasimhappa, the income tax commissioner of Nashik, saw us. We exchanged pleasantries and parted. We proceeded to see the books and to buy cassettes of certain devotional songs. After some time, Sri Narasimhappa came and handed over the passes. Those were the VVIP passes for early morning *Darshan* and told me, 'The passes are meant for me and my family but I am asked to report back at headquarters on urgent work so I am leaving for Nashik". We had a great *Darshan* early in the morning in the front row for the entire morning *Aarti.* This was a great experience and tears rolled out on my cheeks while singing the *Aarti*. This is another occasion when I felt God has invited us without our effort.

Kavi Samrat Sri Visvanatha Satyanarayana

When I was in Vijayawada for personal work, I was staying in Hotel Mamatha. My friend Mr. PVSR Prasad and I went with some friends in the evening and at the end, I went to drop him at his grandfather's house. He invited me into the house. Pawani Sastri, his son who also happened to be a friend also greeted me and invited me inside the house. We spent some time and then they both insisted that I should have dinner with them. Kavi Samrat was also there. I was damn scared sharing dinner with him mainly because the great poet was a very orthodox person. They both said you met him before in Madras when he was felicitated for his Gyan Peeth award and added, "Don't worry, by seeing your mannerism and dictum, nobody will think you are a non-brahmin.' After folding my hands before Kavi Samrat, we sat down on the floor and had dinner, served by Prasad's sister who is Pawani's wife. We were served food in plantain leaves. There was pin-drop silence during the dinner. I passed out in the test and I took leave from there.

Rajaji on his birthday

Nauroji Road in Kilpauk on 10th December 1971. It was a small house where Rajaji was staying and there was no crowd. I went inside with the bouquet. That was his 92nd birthday. Few family members were present there. I introduced myself and explained my admiration for him and his writings. His voice was very feeble. He sat in a chair in the front room. I told him I am the grand-nephew of Late Dr E Raghvendra Rao (ERR). When ERR passed away in 1942, Rajaji offered a post in the government to his son Nageswara Rao Garu, but he rejected it. Later when he was the Home Minister in the Government of India, my maternal uncle Justice R Kausalendra Rao's name was proposed for appointment as a member of the first finance commission. He asked Sri C D Deshmukh, the Finance Minister of India in the cabinet meeting, 'Why did you and how did you select him?'. Sri CD Deshmukh told in the meeting that he knew him personally; he was a product of London School of Economics and he had interviewed him. Rajaji asked, ''Didn't you find a more mature judge in a panel of 84 judges all over the country?' Deshmukh turned serious and said, 'Either he should be in or I should be out'. Rajaji kept quiet. With this background, our family members shared an animosity towards Rajaji, but I admired him. I was regularly reading his front-page article in *Swarajya*. I have bound books of *Swarajya* magazine for over 15 years with me. It is a great treasure for researchers in political sciences. I always remember John Gunther saying, 'Rajaji is endowed with brain all over his body.' He blessed and wished me good luck. Meanwhile, Mrs. Mary Clubwala Jadhav came with a slender garland of roses specially made for him. Rajaji touched her cheeks and blessed her. I took leave from him.

Ashok Kumar, Kishor Kumar, Usha Uthup and S Janaki

On one Sunday, my roommate and I went to Burma Bazaar in Madras. We were trying to buy one Chinese pen and suddenly one open-top Herald car came and stopped by. The boy from the shop went to the car to find out what they wanted to buy. I looked at the car next to the driving seat, The great actor Ashok Kumar was sitting wearing black glasses. After the sales boy left the car, I went to him and greeted him and he started speaking in Hindi with a broad smile. I told him I am a CA student and that I saw his movie *Ashirwad* and liked his song *rail gadi rail gadi*". Perhaps it was the first song composed in rap music in Hindi cinema. He was very happy. I gave him a hundred rupee note on which the white strip used to be there with a watermark and I asked for an autograph. "I will sign but how long you will keep this note" he asked me. I said, "I will preserve it". During those days hundred rupees was big money. He signed it and gave the note back. I kept it for a few months in the purse then exchanged it, forgetting about his autograph.

Kishore Kumar was a craze in Madras with the success of the Hindi movie *Aradhana*. There was a music program of Kishore Kumar arranged by Brahma Gana Sabha in which I was a member. The university centenary hall was the venue. Kishore Kumar was singing some songs with political satire in mind apart from his popular songs. I went up to the stage when he was cracking jokes and requested him to sing a song from the movie, *Teen Deviyan, Khwab ho tum ya koi haqeeqat*'. He asked me whether the Happy song or sad song, I said the sad song. He asked me "Will you dance with me?", I said it is a sad song so no dance. He said, 'After this number, I will sing because I already announced one number and sang the song.' I was excited about my adventure and for his immediate response. Our conversation was in Hindi that too in the mic. Talking in Hindi was not normal in those days in Madras. The next day in my office my senior and grandson of TV Sundaram Iyengar, Mr. SA Krishnan popularly known as Chakrai, who was present in the auditorium told everyone in the office about my encounter with Kishore Kumar on stage. Later I went to an audit of Easun engineering group company. The chief financial officer asked me whether I was the same person who was on stage with Kishore Kumar. I said yes.CA students normally do not indulge in cultural activities because time is precious for them. I always believed one thing: work while you work, enjoy while you enjoy.

One day Usha Iyer's program was conducted in the university's centenary hall; it was a fully crowded program. I really enjoyed her singing. They used to put up sign boards as she was a popular singer in Savera Hotel. 'Remember November is the month of Usha Iyer' (later Usha Uthup). I went up to the stage with a slip requesting her to sing the Hindi movie song *Bindiya Chamkegi.* She agreed and sang the song in her own style, not like Lata Mangeshkar. Nearly three decades after the program, I met her at the Ashoka hotel in Bangalore while she was having her breakfast. I reminded about her program in Madras. She really enjoyed talking with me and invited me to the evening program. I went, since I was staying in the same hotel. She announced my name on the stage and said 'A fan of mine is attending my program after 30 years'.

One day in Bangalore I was staying in hotel Atria. I went down to the dining hall to have my dinner. That evening there was heavy gale and rain in the city with a number of trees falling and disrupting the traffic. When I went down, I saw a group of nearly ten members sitting on the big table and at the head of the table, I found Srimati S. Janaki, the most popular playback singer of South India. I occupied my table. Later, I went to that table and said, *namaste*. She also returned back with *namaste*. Then I started conversing and she immediately got up from her seat with a lot of respect and I requested her to sit but she denied. An extra chair was drawn by the steward. I told her that I am a great fan of her songs right from the Telugu movie, *Muripinche Muvvalu* and told her that I belong to Repalle from where she also comes. She told me that because of the disastrous rain the original program for which she came for singing was postponed to next day evening. That's the reason why she is in the hotel and relaxing with local relatives. I also told her about some of her biographical details I read in Shri Kompella Ravichander's book *Gnapakalu*. She said that she has no idea about the book but she enjoyed talking to me. After she finished her dinner, she signalled to me that she was leaving. Immediately I got up and went to her and thanked her for the time she spent. I was really surprised; she was very unassuming and friendly to talk to even though I was a stranger. Great people are simple.

Jayalalitha, Satyajit Ray, Tony Greig and K Jaggaiah

One day I was attending a dance program of Vempati Chinna Satyam's troupe in the Music Academy Hall in Madras. After an hour I came out to have a cigarette. Jayalalitha was standing out in the lounge, waiting for her car to come. No one was there in the vicinity. We smiled at each other. I think it was in 1972- 73; she was still in the cinemas. I told her I liked her movie *Aame Evaru*. She smiled again and her blue coloured Plymouth car came and she left. But I can never forget her captivating smile.

One day my roommates PVSR Prasad, Nagesh and I were on a holiday in Bombay since Nagesh's uncle Viswanath, an engineer in Sagar Samrat was on leave and his flat was vacant in the Santacruz area. When we visited the Gateway of India, we went to Taj Mahal hotel, now Taj Palace and visited "Shamiyana" the coffee shop (now also with the same name). We came out after having a cup of coffee and Tony Greig, the captain of the England team touring India with some of his team members was in the lounge of the hotel. All of us were overwhelmed. Immediately I approached him and asked for his autograph on a hundred rupee note. He smiled and signed.

After setting up my practice in Hyderabad KK, MARK Raju and I went to attend the *filmotsav* at Madras in January 1978. As a part of the festival, an exhibition was conducted in Taj Coromandel hotel. We visited the exhibition where I was talking to Sri Rallabandi Kameswara Rao, a Shakespearean drama artist and son of my father's friend Sri Rallabandi Subba Rao Garu. Suddenly I found Sri Satyajit Ray. I approached him and said *namaste*. He greeted me. I told him I saw the first two cinemas in, Apu Trilogy. I further told him the screening of Bengali cinemas is a rare thing in Madras. He nodded his head. A sturdy person with sharp looks and he said thanks. KK was watching me from a distance talking to Satyajit Ray with ease.

Same day evening Shri DK Rao, CEO of the Simpson group invited me, KK, Mark Raju and the famous Telugu film actor and former MP, Sri K Jaggayya for dinner at Madras Gymkhana Club. The previous day, Shri Jaggayya arrived at our hotel and had a long discussion with KK. KK invited him to join Congress, led by Srimati Indira Gandhi and contest for Lok Sabha. He will be appointed as minister for information and broadcasting. That was the purpose of the meeting. He was a member of Lok Sabha 1967-72 representing Ongole on a congress ticket.

I was not the part of the meeting. The result was Jaggayya refused to join the party. He said, 'I don't want to join the party of a person who has imposed an emergency in the country'. He contested in 1979 on a different ticket and lost the election, which is another story. In the evening, all of us met at Madras Gymkhana Club. We had an interesting discussion on Telugu literature specially the colloquial language used in Andhra and Telangana regions which continued till midnight. We finally concluded on the note that language used in Telangana was real Telugu and was less corrupt by the Sanskrit language. During the discussion, from the way Sri Jaggayya was quoting various authors, I realised that he was a voracious reader. Then my friends told me that he has a good library. I used to know that he was a great actor with a thundering voice. It was a great experience to know that there was a great scholar in the cinema actor.

Compose and Click

"Photography has been my hobby since my high school days. I wanted to pursue it even as a career. It helped me to develop an eye for understanding beauty and how to frame it through the lens."

I was in class four in school (9 years old) when my grandfather decided to have a family photo at our home in Vellaturu. The photographer was brought from Tenali to do the service. He brought a big camera with four legs and covered himself in a black cloth behind the viewfinder. We were all sitting before our imposing verandah with two large pillars and steps. He asked us not to move a bit when he was clicking. It was all amusing to me. The group photo came out well. It aroused my curiosity to know about photography even though I had seen it in high schools at Addada and Tadepalli in Krishna district where my father was the headmaster and encouraged photography as an extracurricular activity. He even allowed to build a dark room for photo processing. For my 10th birthday, my maternal grandmother Shrimati Kokila Bai gave me a gift of rupees 25 and asked my father to buy a camera for me. "Sure Shot" was the camera made in lightweight with bakelite material. I remember Patel India was distributing this camera and view masters that was the first Indian camera with fixed focus. Later Agfa company introduced 'Click III' into the market. Today many photographers do not remember these Indian products. The camera was costed only rupees 25 but the roll was for rupees four for 12 photographs. However, for developing and printing additional four rupees were charged. That is how I have learnt and experimented on photography.

I used to wander in our mango and lemon gardens and agriculture fields to take photographs. Results were encouraging.. I was the only person among the 2000 people in the village who owned a camera; it was thrilling for me as a boy. All our farmworkers and farm managers were happy to see their photographs and their agriculture operations photographed. Then I asked my sister Vijayalakshmi Ramakrishnan to bring a pròfessional camera for me from the USA. In 1971 she bought a "Yashica 635" at a cost of $80. I started understanding the nuances like focal length, light metre, composition, depth of field etc and clicked photos.

In 1974, my first photograph was published in *Caravan*, an English magazine. Another was published in 1975 January in *Andhra Prabha* weekly *Sankranti* special issue. Later, I had sent my photographs as entries in amateur photographers' exhibition held at Hyderabad where I received a consolation prize in 1975 for my Whirlpool. It was shot in *Sangam Jagarlamudi* where we went for a photoshoot along with my friends.

I always carried my Yashica on my tours and got good results, especially nature photography. My professional studies as a CA student became a priority for me. After passing the chartered accountancy and setting up my own practice in 1977 which became a greater responsibility for me, photography took a backseat. But it remained as a hobby.

Photography has undergone rapid changes. Technology enabled the field to expand in every direction. Slowly manual photography turned into digital photography. The digital cameras were also operating on rolls with automatic and semi-automatic settings and many features are in-built in such cameras for better results. But the manual camera like my Yashica always gave very good satisfaction with 120 or 35mm rolls; the results are equally comparable to digital cameras. In 1982, I bought a full-frame digital camera operating on 35mm rolls Yashica 108. My brand loyalty to Yashica remained. The results were excellent but processing of rolls became very expensive mostly because of imported chemicals and processing equipment. Then I started using full digital cameras without rolls, a Canon 450D, a lightweight camera in 2005. The digital camera reduced processing costs and there was flexibility in number of shots; especially when it comes to deleting what's not required and processing only the ones you want to really print. It is also advantageous to send these digital photos through electronic media. There is the scope for editing a photograph, which is not up to the mark. With this, the art of photography remained as a digital exercise rather than a mental exercise. The role of a photographer is reduced. The thrill of waiting to see what is going to come after the process is gone. Speed in life and speed of results ultimately bid adieu to creativity. No doubt "Ansel Adams" can be created but digitally.

Later I acquired a Canon 5D full frame camera with other gear required to make short films. I have been using lenses 55 - 250mm and 70- 500mm and 55 -400mm. These lenses I used mainly for wildlife photography. I made my trips to Kumarakom in Kerala, Ranganathittu and Malavalli in Karnataka, Bharatpur in Rajasthan and Sewri mudflats in Mumbai. The results were very good. My desire to become a professional photographer remained unfulfilled, although my photographs looked very professional.

As a student, I was always inspired by Raghu Rai and had often waited to see the photograph of the week in *Illustrated Weekly* of India. Raghu Rai was equally good in outdoor and indoor photography. I always used to tell my father that had I not joined CA I would have surpassed Raghu Rai's photography. In the days of black and white photography, Raghu Rai was the king of photographers in the media.

I became a member of AP Photographic Society when it had just begun with the leadership of Sri Bhagavan Das IAS. But I never found extra time to participate in its activities. With all the photographs from manual to digital that I clicked, I wanted to make a one-man show and that remained a distant dream. I published over 40 photographs of birds alone in two volumes of my book, *My Views and Reviews*. After the conclusion of each article on an industry, I published photograph of a bird to remind us of our duty to conserve the environment. Out of many workshops I attended on photography, one conducted by Atul Kasbekar, was interesting. I am possessive of his certificate.

Life is a Cocktail

"Having interests and dabbling a bit in different lines of activity in addition to regular vocation made life interesting. Born in a country where the traditions, dressing, food habits, festivals and folk music are different in each region pushed me to explore."

Music and Dance

I have been interested in art, music, architecture and cinema since my childhood, mainly because of my parents. My mother was a trained singer. In those days it was a taboo for ladies to get trained in singing. Her father Sri Boppana Somayya Garu encouraged her and she was trained by Sri Parvathaneni Veeraiah, a fourth generation direct disciple of Sri ThyagaRaja with Guru Parampara of Walajapet Venkatrama Bhagavatar, Thiruvottiyur Thyagayya, Susarla Dakshinamurthy (Senior). He was the first *Asthana Vidwan* of the government of AP after Independence. He was a great freedom fighter who led the no-tax campaign in Pedanandipadu near Chirala along with the Chirala perala movement led by Andhra Ratna Sri Duggirala Gopala Krishnayya garu. Her father organised teaching music at home in Tenali for mother. Others who also joined her were Shrimati Sarojini Garu, the daughter of Tripuraneni Ramaswamy Chowdary, a barrister and social reformer and Bayammagaru Garu, niece of Dr Vullakki, a famous doctor educated in Edinburgh. She gave her concert before the invited gathering at home when her father hosted a dinner in honour of Sir AP Patro, the education minister in Madras province.

My mother had a beautiful voice but lacked the knack for singing in high pitch up to the mark. This is my observation of her singing in her fifties. She was singing at home and I used to follow her and sing along. Her favourite kritis of Thyagaraja were, " *Evarani Nirnayinchedi ra* in Poornachandrika Ragam, *Santamu leka soukhyamu ledu* in Sama Ragam, *Pakkala nilabadi in kharaharapriya, Vandanamu raghunandana in Sahana Ragam Raghuvamsa sudhambudhi* in kadanakuthuhalam.

We used to have a gramophone and a battery-operated radio (Mullard from Germany) in the 1950s. I had the advantage of following radio programs along with her. My father used to sing *Ramadas Keerthanas* and *Enki Patalu*. Although his voice was not so musical, his expression of bhakti as well as grief was parallel with the lyrics and that's how my music appreciation started. Mother was a fan of DK Pattammal and Brinda and Mukta duo. I used to pick up singing by listening to my mother and All India Radio with melody but without grammar. I used to follow light music programs in All India Radio. Many cinema playback artists started their careers in AIR. We used to follow artists like Jikki, Ghantasala and M S Rama Rao who sang in light music which are not cinema songs. My father used to like Bengaluru Rangamani Ammal and her song *Muruga Muruga*.

I used to sing Rao Balasaraswathi's Gopala krishnudu nallana Gokulamlo PaluThellana. Nayanamma (my paternal grandmother) used to listen to Bhakti Ranjani, a devotional music program in AIR. I used to follow the programs and sing Sadasiva Brahmendra Keerthanalu, Tattvams, and Ramadas Keerthanas.

I am a great fan of Balamuralikrishna and MS Subbulakshmi. As my education was in villages there was no Guru to teach me music. I was not encouraged also though I had the god-given gift of a reasonably good voice.

A friend of my father Kodali Uma Maheswara Rao Garu, a Hindi Pandit associated with Praja Natyamandali always used to appreciate and encourage my singing and used to write to my father inquiring whether I am singing or not. Now I am fulfilling the desire of singing by singing in karaoke programs in Secunderabad Club and a couple of hotels. It is quite satisfying when many from the audience come and appreciate my rendering personally. I have installed a small equipment at home which is connected to my home theatre. It helps me sing at least once in a week.

During the project appraisal meetings for the condom project, Dr Reddy's friend Mr M A Aziz of Nellore used to meet me. He was the secretary of Andhra club and a small-time cinema producer, who had produced *Kiladi Krishnudu*, a Telugu movie.. Impressed by my singing skills, he said one day that he will get a screen test and introduce me as a playback singer like he did Vijaya Shanti as the heroine. I never took it seriously and never pursued it.

The singing gene continued in our family. My son Sai Thejasvee is a good singer and a trained salsa dancer. He also attended a course in Arizona State University on movie direction and editing, and directed two advertisement movies for start-ups.

As a child, I was taken to a famous dance program conducted in Vijaya Talkies in Vijayawada (perhaps 1954-55). That was the first dance program I had ever witnessed and that too of great Balasaraswati (Balamma). I had attended the first music concert of Smt M S Subbulakshmi in Guntur when she sang for the benefit of Loyola Public School. When I was in high school, I participated in a children's programme in All India Radio Vijayawada and sang Rayaprolu Subba rao's. '*Eh Desamegina*'. Kumari Vinjamuri Lakshmi who conducted the programme appreciated my singing.

After completing my college studies, I went to Madras for my chartered accountancy. I became a member of Brahma Gana Sabha at Madras 1971 to 74 and enjoyed music as well as dance programs, performances of great artists in the country like Pandit Ravi Shankar (sitar), Anand Shankar, (fusion music) Madurai Mani Iyer, Semmangudi, M S Subbulakshmi, M Bala Muralikrishna, John Higgins, (vocal), Chitti Babu, Balachander, (veena), Yamini Krishnamurthy, Hema Malini, Sanjukta Panigrahi,(dance), and TR Mahalingam (flute). After relocating to Hyderabad, I became a life member of the South India Cultural Association (SICA) and enjoyed performances of later generation artists like Shubha Mudgal, Aruna Sairam, Hyderabad sisters, Hariprasad Chaurasia, Pandit Shivkumar Sharma and his son, KJ Yesudas and dancer Shobhana. It has been a great experience to see such top artists performing on stage. I enjoyed a music and dance programme in the Opera house in Times Square in New York along with Rama and Mukund, my cousin.

Though I am not trained in music, I have learned to appreciate music and dance through my parents. This encouraged me to attend the performances of great artists whenever I can. Reading about them and their efforts to excel inspired me besides just gaining pleasure. In the bargain, I am trying to understand a bit about *ragas* in music and different dance forms in India. I always remember the humble words of Srimati D K Pattammal: Music is like a big ocean, I know only a bit. (In Tamil, *Sangeetham oru Periya samudram ennaku konchem terium*)

Cinema and Film Appreciation

Many people think cinema is commercial and not art, but I always argue that it is the greatest art where acting, dialogue delivery, cinematography, music, dance, lyrics synchronise to make the scene perfect. Screenplay is the back-office work. So much of planning and detailing goes into making a cinema. My parents always used to encourage me to watch the movies since I could pick up the tune just by listening once. We also purchased cinema songs' books which were available outside the theatre. After picking up the tune I used to sing with the help of the lyrics in the books. In those days there were no tape recorders or *Vividh Bharati* for cinema music. We used to go to Vijayawada and Tenali for watching the movies and catch the last bus or connecting train even before the completion of the movie. When we were watching the movie *Mughal-E Ajam*, we left the theatre for catching the bus after the song *zindabad -zindabad*. We couldn't watch the rest of the 20 minutes of the movie.

My uncle, Kutumba Rao Garu was an advocate for many prominent persons in the film field. He was also financing cinema producers. It is not out of place to mention that when my mother sold her six acres of land at Pedamaddali village, the proceeds of Rs 18000, in 1950 came handy to finance and complete the famous Telugu film, P*atala Bhiravi*. He took me to watch *Seeta*

Rama Kalyanam, a blockbuster of yesteryears for the first day first show. The movie started late because Sri Trivikram Rao, the producer and brother of NT Rama Rao, the hero of the movie arrived late to switch on the projector. He introduced me to him and told that I am a good singer. There was a huge gathering and traffic jam thinking NTR was present. Such was his popularity and mass appeal.

My father used to explain me about costumes, settings, natural scenes, etc after the movie We used to watch hindi movies of great directors like Asif, Shantharam, Guru Dutt, Bimal Roy, Mehaboob Khan in Hindi. English movies like *Ten Commandments, Benhur, Oliver, Cleopatra, My Fair Lady* together. When he came to see me in Madras, I booked tickets for *Cromwell.* He explained to me the history behind the movie, the revolution in the country, the establishment of parliamentary democracy, its failure and restoring the monarchy back.

With this background and knowledge, I launched a film club in the name "Sight and Sound Academy". We invited Nimai Ghosh for the inauguration and held a one-day course in film appreciation for which Aravindan was invited. We screened foreign language films in a mini theatre in Ravindra Bharathi. I was the vice president and former Director-General of Police, Sri M V Narayana Rao IPS was the president, Ramakrishnam Raju of Ramachandra tools was the secretary. After a couple of years, its pace plummeted because the secretary was not co-ordinating, though he initiated the activities with great enthusiasm. I could not pursue further as the organisation became defunct.

I wrote a script for a short film as an entry in amateur film festival in Pune. I was also associated in the production of the movie

Nimajjanam at the time of story selection and was involved in scriptwriting. Shri K Keshava Rao was the producer along with Shri Krishna Rao Keshav and B S Narayana, was its director. The movie was awarded with Rajat Kamal and its heroine, Sharada received the, Urvashi Award. Chakrapani. It's hero is still in touch with me for his tax matters. There was a preview in Sarathi Studios attended by all the bigwigs including Chandrasekhar erstwhile hero and producer of Hindi movies, *Cha Cha Cha* and *Street singer. Nimajjanam* was not commercially successful; still KK proposed a partnership with 10 partners including me, contributing Rs 1,00,000 each to produce Art cinemas, the banner's name was Viplav Art Productions. That was the time when Parallel Cinema movement was catching up with directors like Sham Benegal, M S Sathyu, Basu Chatterjee, and Mrinal Sen. He was also on the National Film Awards jury when I K Gujral was the information and broadcasting minister. After KK became busy in politics and became a cabinet minister in AP, there was no one to lead the Viplav Art. It was a no starter.

Paintings

Navrang Chitra Kala Niketan (1968- 69) was an art promoting institution and it was set up in our village Vellaturu by Sri Vellaturi Purnananda Sarma, a famous painter. He used to conduct international competitions in drawing and painting among children. Entries used to come from various countries. He was known for his paintings on rural life. He also painted a portrait of my paternal grandfather Nagabhushanam Garu, an oil painting on canvas which adorns the walls of our village Kacheri. My father made me a patron of this institution. That is how I started appreciating art from the age of 17.

In later life, I visited a number of museums in the country to see works of art and great masters in India. Jehangir Art Gallery, National Museum of Modern Art New Delhi, museums in Baroda, Jaipur, Calcutta, Trivandrum, Salarjung Museum Hyderabad, Jaganmohan Palace in Mysore were some of them to specially mention. It is a treat to see the paintings belonging to various schools of art Mughal, Bikaneri, Rajput from Rajasthan, Pahadi, Kangra from Himachal region, Cherial, Nirmal, and Kalamkari, from Telangana and Andhra Pradesh, Tanjore and Mysore paintings from South, Deccani paintings from Golconda. Paintings in India evolved over centuries and with influences in and outside the country. I saw paintings during the East India company era in the Jehangir art gallery, paintings of contemporary artists like Jaimini Roy, Abanindranath Tagore, and Nandalal Bose in Kolkata and Trivandrum art galleries. I also saw some of the good paintings of Amrita Shergill in hotel Centaur in Bombay whenever I was staying. Raja Ravi Varma's paintings in Baroda are more in number than in Trivandrum gallery. His painting *Poverty* in Trivandrum art gallery is a classic and has also received an international award. Jaganmohan Palace displays S L Haldankar's *Lady with the Lamp*, which is also a very interesting painting.

The houses in Rajasthan and Gujarat were fully covered with murals and when I saw those houses, I felt that art is part of our life in India. Murals and frescoes in temples is another work of art encouraged in the country by various dynasties of rulers. Even the cave paintings of the prehistoric era can be seen in some parts of the country. In Ajanta and Ellora, paintings belonging to the Buddhist period are still a delight to watch and enjoy.

Meeting artists is another experience, when my father took me to meet Sri S. Sanjeev Dev, a great painter of Andhra in Tummapudi near Tenali in his house. In my later life, I met his son, a well-known agri-economist, Shri Mahendra Dev with Dr N Bhaskar Rao, my friend. Shri Sanjeev Dev was a disciple of Nicholas Roerich, an internationally famous painter. I met Sri Surya Prakash, another well-known painter and brother of Sri Veerabhadra Rao, a police officer and my friend. His "pool of lilies" reminds me of Claude Monet. I went to Siddipet on an official visit. I met Shri Rajayya, a painter. He is a fine example of how lack of publicity and exposure keeps an artist in oblivion. He presented me with a painting which he made.

Ilango and his bulls are popular like M F Hussain and his horses. It was a pleasure to meet Ilango in the Administrative Staff College of India where he was conducting an exhibition. One night I was in the poolside restaurant in hotel Banjara in Hyderabad. I saw barefooted MF Hussain on another table. He was in the company of two young girls. I was inquisitive and followed him after they finished dinner, along with my friend. He reached his abode in Masab Tank and the girls left in the car. I felt bad for my unnecessary curiosity in my twenties as a bachelor. Later I met MF Husain in Cuffe Parade in his flat where my friend BV Goud was his immediate neighbour. I met sculptors like CSN Patnaik and Ravindra Reddy belonging to two generations and who used different mediums for sculpting. Ravindra Reddy is the son-in-law of Sri P Janardhan Reddy of Warangal, our client. I met him on a number of occasions. He is a very simple and unassuming person in spite of his international fame. I have continued my love for art and I always seek to know about the feelings that these paintings and sculpture evoke. There is so much sculpture and architecture in India, especially temple architecture, which I had the opportunity to visit in my travels with a specific interest in various architectural schools in different periods.

Paintings and Sculpture in USA and Europe

The story of seeing paintings abroad started with my visit to The Institute of Art in Chicago when I attended an international conference. It was continued later with Metropolitan Museum of Art in New York which I visited along with my cousins, Murali from Connecticut and Mukund from New York. The museum possesses collections which gives the idea of the evolution of paintings and sculptures in various civilizations. I also visited the Museum of Fine Arts in Boston. Dr Visvendra Rao, my cousin, took me and Rama to the Asian Museum of Arts in San Francisco. My sister Vijayalakshmi Ramakrishnan took me and Rama to the Natural History Museum in Rapid City.

Sai took us to the Legion of Honour Museum. Tapasvi and I visited the Computer History Museum. The urge to see and learn never stopped. I visited the Science and Technology Museum and China Art Museum in Shanghai along with Avinash. I also visited the Astronomy Museum in Chicago extending my antennas to other areas of knowledge.

The experience of seeing the art and paintings of many centuries in Rome, Florence, Venice and Paris is the greatest in my life. Seeing great works of Masters like Vincent Van Gogh, Rembrandt, Michelangelo, Leonardo da Vinci, and Renoir and other artists like Caravaggio, Botticelli, Raphael, Titian are only a few names to mention. I never understood Picasso and modern art.

Be it impressionism, post-impressionism, expressionism, realism, surrealism, symbolism, naturalism, cubism and different types of paintings like portraits, landscapes, seascapes, still life; whether they are with watercolours, oil on canvas, pastel, or pencil sketches of great painters, their styles, colour choice and their brush strokes are so versatile. I really liked the brush strokes of Edgar Degas' in his paintings on ballet and dancers with their movements in a series of paintings. I found something unique was pointillism which I found really impressive. *Sailing Boats and Pine Trees* by Paul Signac and *Landscape with Goats* by Henry-Edmund Cross are rare in their own way. Van Gogh also followed this style in some of his paintings. I had the chance of seeing an exhibition in Rome where I saw two good paintings in pointillism: *By the Window* by Achillelauge and *Portrait of the Violinist* by Theo Van Ryssel Berghe. These two looked like mosaics on canvas to me. In Paris, I could see the exclusive collection of Claude Monet on large Canvas.

Sculptures of Bernini are really mind-boggling. I liked his *David* more than Michelangelo's, may be because of Baroque art. Canova is another sculptor whose work I can never forget. The bronze equestrian statue of Emperor Marcus Aurelius is again a tribute to art and metallurgy which dates back to 170 to 180 AD.

Auguste Rodin's bronze sculptures in Paris are modern in style and are beautiful. I saw some of his sculptures on the Stanford campus. Sculptures and his collection of art pieces in Paris mostly belong to 19th and 20th centuries.

Since 1980, I have possessed a collection of Masterminds in Arts in six volumes and Encyclopaedia of museums in 10 volumes on the well-known museums of the world and their collection of art pieces which provided a lot of information on art. I am quite happy that I could visit museums like the Metropolitan Museum of Art, Museum of Fine Arts in Boston, The Institute of Art in Chicago, Museums in Vatican City, and Louvre in Paris. It was only possible because of Sai and Anusha's (his wife) planning. Sai proposed to visit the British Museum in London and the National Gallery in Washington to quench our thirst for seeing and appreciating art.

Travels

My mother used to say, 'Reading makes a man complete and travel makes a man perfect.' This always rings in my mind.. Since childhood I have been travelling with my parents for family functions, because my relatives are spread from Bilaspur in Madhya Pradesh to Coimbatore in Tamil Nadu. Later when I was doing my CA articles, I was travelling on audit work. Whenever I was on an audit tour, I used to visit the nearby places for sightseeing. This continued throughout my professional life. Some of them to mention are Chittira Art Gallery, in Trivandrum, Grand Anicut built by Karikala Cholan near Trichy, Vivekananda Rock Memorial at Kanyakumari, Murugan Temple in Palani ,Victoria Memorial in Kolkata, Yercaud a small hill station near Salem, Morni hills near Chandigarh, Sabarmati Ashram in Ahmedabad, Gandhi Memorial at Mani Bhavan in Mumbai, Rabindranath Tagore's House, and Netaji Subhas Chandra Bose's house in Kolkata, Cherrapunji, Shillong, magnificent Taj Mahal in Agra, and many more.

The primary aim of travelling and sightseeing is to understand the local conditions including nature, climate, people, their dress, food, and style of living etc. The secondary aim is to understand styles of architecture, town planning, flora and fauna. After our marriage and birth of Sai, we visited Jammu and Srinagar, Pehalgam, Gulmarg etc. in Kashmir. We enjoyed seeing the cottage in Pehalgaon where the popular Hindi song, *Hum tum ek kamare me bandh ho aur Chabee khojaye* was shot. We were also elated to see a good library in the temple of Sri Rama and family deity of Kashmir Royal family in Jammu.

We also visited Patiala and Shimla when the kids were very young. The visit to Patiala palace museum and National Sports Academy was interesting. We enjoyed the trip in the company of Col KKD Prasad's family and his daughters Neeta and Priyanka. After children reached the age of 10 and 12, I started taking the family on summer visits to Ooty, Kodaikanal, Munnar, Goa in winter, and Kerala. When children started writing their competitive exams and pursuing higher studies, our annual sojourn ceased. We always used to visit the important places in a particular state where the hill station is situated mainly to make children understand the local conditions and people. Once Sai, who was still studying came from the USA, we went to Goa in winter. When both Tapasvi and Sai came from USA, we all went to Kerala. Sai enjoyed the Keralite cuisine, and its nature, especially the stay in the houseboat which was exclusively booked for us. One crew member suddenly plunged into the lake and caught large-sized tiger prawns. I enjoyed my drink on the deck along with the fresh tiger prawns caught in the lake and cooked by the chef in the boat. We enjoyed *Kalaripayattu*, a native martial art show. We went to Varkala Kovalam Beach and Thekkady. Sai went to Kerala again on his way to Lakshadweep for his honeymoon trip.

A trip to Goa included visiting Aihole, Badami caves, and Pattadakal. Badami caves are huge and witness to Jains, Buddhists, and later Hindus, occupying them and also for sculpture of different religions. Apsidal temple of Durga is interesting in Aihole because of its totally different design and style. Pattadakal seems to be the mother of temple architecture in the South since we can see different styles of temple architecture. In our trip to Goa, we visited the Doodh Sagar waterfalls. It is very picturesque. However, the waterfalls at Kuntala in Telangana are more enjoyable. On our trip to Ooty, we also visited Brindavan Gardens near Krishna Raja Sagar Dam which is a great gift of Sir M Visvesvaraya and subsequent *diwans* of Mysore state to this Nation. Mysore Palace which was built over eight years is inarguably splendorous. Jaganmohan Palace preserves many art treasures in Mysore. We also visited Gol Gumbaz in Bijapur which is the largest dome in the world with 144 feet outer diameter, which is built without any support built in 1626 to 1656. It is known for its acoustics and engineering. The dome at St Peter's Basilica is about 142 ft diameter which we visited recently in December 2019. On that trip, we visited Pantheon in Rome with a dome of 142 ft diameter and Duomo in Florence with a dome of 138.5 ft diameter.

In our trip to Kodaikanal and Munnar, we visited Thanjavur Saraswathi Mahal which preserves over 60000 volumes of books, including books in palmyra leaves in Telugu, Tamil and Sanskrit belonging to the 16th and 17th centuries. It was very interesting though their preservation may not be as per international standards. Thanjavur was ruled by Telugu royal generations like Vijayanagar kings and Madurai Nayaka kings. Finally, with the reign of Chhatrapati Shivaji there came a Maratha king as ruler after preventing the invasion on Thanjavur. Even now we find many Maratha families settled in Thanjavur for centuries. Thyagaraja, the great composer and maestro in Carnatic music belonged to Thanjavur in his times though his family migrated from a village called Kakarla in Prakasam district of Andhra Pradesh. We made it a point to visit Thiruvaiyaru where a temple is built for him. The tallest Gopuram of Thanjavur Brihadeeswara temple with the tall Shiva Lingam is imposing and an engineering marvel during the regime of Chola Kings, though the layout looks like a Buddhist arama and even some ruins of Buddhist sculptures were found in excavations during certain renovation a few years ago in Thanjavur. Tapasvi wonders even now about the building of Brihadeeswara temple with the tallest Gopuram in the country (210ft) and mounting the crowning dome (as per J C Harley in his book, *The Art and Architecture of Indian Subcontinent* it is a single stone with a diameter of twenty-five and a half feet and the estimated weight of 80 tons) when there were no material handling equipments.

When we visited Madurai temple, the market nearby was very interesting with a variety of articles than a present-day mall. Tapasvi and Sai bought a number of board games there. I was really amazed at Madurai's town planning and the planning and structure of Thirumalai Nayak Palace built between 1629 and 1636. We proceeded to Tiruchirappalli to see the Grand Anicut, an earthen dam with stones called, *Kallanai* to regulate water from five streams built by Karikala Cholan in 2nd century A.D, a well thought of irrigation project. Srirangam temple near Trichy is the biggest temple complex in India. It is a fortified township. I am really impressed with it's architecture. That was my third trip to Srirangam. Whenever I was visiting that part of Tamil Nadu, I never missed the temple visit. On my first visit in 1972, I saw a ceiling of a Mandapam (hall) fully painted with the artwork of Ramayana and the description was in Telugu language of Vijayanagar period. I was disappointed in my third trip after 15 years as it was totally peeled off. I wanted to show the children the Telugu inscriptions detailing Ramayana. It was a very painful experience and it is a fine example of how art is neglected in India. Similar such murals I saw in Met pally temple in Nalgonda district Telangana are also in a poor condition. It is a great misfortune that we have no respect for art whereas in the west, private trusts, business houses and public organisations take care of such treasure.

Rameswaram temple is awesome with huge corridors and beautiful sculptures. Dhanush Koti beach near Rameswaram is really lively. We all visited Kanyakumari where you can see the water and sands of Bay of Bengal, Arabian Sea, and Indian Ocean distinctly. It is a great site to enjoy the sunset. Vivekananda Rock Memorial is so serene that I even meditated in the basement hall. That was my second visit to the place after 20 years.

In another visit to India, Sai, Anusha, Rama and I visited Madras to attend Ranganathan's daughter Satwika's wedding and stayed in Mahabalipuram in Radissons Beach resort. Anusha always reminisces the stay in Mahabalipuram. We had seen the Shore temples, Rock-cut caves and sculptures on rocks there. They are quite similar to those in Kailasa temple in Maharashtra. The sculpture, especially on great relief has Roman influence but, different from the Gandhara School of Art in my opinion. Some new stone reliefs surfaced after the receding Tsunami in 2004. What is more interesting in Mahabalipuram is the structure on the tallest hillock where they used to create fire with some local material for sparking flames to identify the light for the sailing ships. Hats off to their imaginary and engineering skills. A modern lighthouse was built near there in recent years.

In my official trips, I usually stayed in Bombay and Delhi for nearly four decades and especially between 1983 and 93, once a week. Other cities I had a stay include Ahmedabad, Jaipur, Chandigarh, Lucknow, Kolkata, Pune, Bhubaneswar, Trivandrum, Guwahati and Shillong.

On one of my trips to Calcutta, I visited Raja Mullik's Palace which my mother used to talk about and his collection of exotic birds. She, along with her aunts, stayed in Raja Malik's guest house in the same compound. The guest house was not functional when I visited. Andhra Bank arranged the meeting for me with Raja Mullik's son. He personally took me around the Palace and the collections. He told me that in spite of many restrictions he was still importing birds with the permission of the Government of India He also mentioned that it is difficult to get permissions. Tagore's House and Library are also interesting. I have one photograph of Tagore when he visited Indian students in Oxford. They requested me to send that, I thought I will give a framed one, which never happened. I visited Gandhi's Sabarmati Ashram in Ahmedabad and Gandhi's memorial Mani Bhavan in Mumbai.

Trip to Shillong and Cherrapunji from Guwahati was really a memorable trip. I considered myself lucky when we planned to visit the Kamakhya temple on Vijayadasami day but seeing bloodstains flowing along with the rainwater, the result of animal slaughter in the premises pained me and felt we were living in a primitive society.. I took my partner Shri Avinash Jain with me who belongs to a non-violent religion. I was embarrassed and apologized to him. He understood and said, 'ok sir,' simply. Even watching the river Brahmaputra from the top of the temple premises was really frightening unlike river Sarayu in Ayodhya in its full form, which was calm and peaceful, when I visited in my trip to Lucknow. The trip from Guwahati to Cherrapunji via Shillong is good but only after reaching Cherrapunji, the hill looked like clean shaved without trees. It is a clear case of how the nature is manipulated. The attraction in Cherrapunji is caves formed out of stalagmite and two waterfalls NavKhali 1120 feet height which is the highest in the country and seven sisters with the height of 1033 feet. In USA, I enjoyed the nature at its best in Tapasvi's driving, when we visited Sedona and Grand Canyon and spent a day with the family, travelled through Apache trail in Arizona state and reached Roosevelt Dam. We clicked some good snaps in Grand Canyon.

On three of my official trips, Rama also accompanied me. In one of my trips to Delhi, we went to Agra to see Fatehpur Sikri and Taj Mahal. I was searching for traces of Hindu architecture and symbols since I read P N Oak's book on Taj Mahal. I did the same even when we visited Red Fort in Delhi since I read an article published in *Illustrated Weekly* of India written by P N Oak on Red Fort. There is some amount of truth that the structures belonged to the Hindu architecture. For Rama, Delhi was not new, only Swaminarayan Mandir was an addition in recent times for her to see. I could not go because of my work. She also visited Calcutta along with me. I could not go out because of my work. She felt happy to see the Kali temple, Hare Krishna Mandir, Ramakrishna Math, Mother Teresa's home and the house of Subhas Chandra Bose.

Shri MS Kapoor, the chairman of Vijaya Bank, personally invited me with family for the Platinum jubilee celebrations of Vijaya Bank. A number of dignitaries like Maharana of Udaipur, Deve Gowda, the former prime minister were participating along with us and many other film personalities from Mumbai. Sridevi was one of them. Sri Ratnakar Hegde, the GM of the bank (later ED of Union Bank of India) took me and Rama to Sridevi and Boney Kapoor and introduced me as Statutory Auditor of the bank. She was so humble and spoke with a lot of respect, I told her that I have been watching her movies right from, *Badi Panthulu* in which she acted as a child artiste. I was impressed with her conduct in the meeting and celebrations. I was thrilled to see B Saroja Devi who was a popular heroine when I was in my youth, sitting next to my row, in the meeting.

Travelling outside India includes an international conference in Shanghai where I presented a paper. In another international conference, I participated at Chicago. Both were the conferences of members of Leading Edge Alliance, an association of international accounting firms. I travelled from Shanghai to Beijing along with Avinash, our partner, in a fast train which is the second-fastest travelling at 420 kilometre speed, the first being Shanghai to Maglev at 430 kilometres per hour. China's development was really astonishing. After seeing Shanghai, the business capital of China, I felt that New York was nothing.

Railway stations in China are cleaner and more modern than some of the airports in the USA. In China, poverty was also visible with beggars flocking around Buddha's temple. We visited the Great Wall of China, one of the seven wonders of the world. I saw the Colosseum in Rome, another wonder. It is a colossal built-in brick and mortar around 70 century AD. I saw The Leaning Tower of Pisa in Italy, another wonder on my recent trip to Europe in December 2019 along with Rama and Sai's family by travelling from Florence in "Frecciarossa" 1000, the fourth fastest train in the world.

My first travel outside India was to Bahrain for meeting the investors for OCTL public issue and a trip to Thailand on exploring markets for La Mansion Granites. In both the trips, I was accompanied by the managing directors of the companies. My first trip to USA was to Detroit and Houston for holding discussions with Karmanos Cancer Institute and Baker Hughes on collaboration matters. It was a short trip of one week.

For both official and personal travel and sightseeing trips, I always prepared an itinerary and some notes before the visits about the importance and history of the places. This made me enjoy the tour. The only thing I was not particular about was food, as I am not a great lover of food.

I am lucky to have many opportunities, to explore things whether it is music, dance, photography, art, architecture, culture or nature.

WHAT LIFE HAS TAUGHT ME

"Life is a flowing stream. Learning is a sailing boat. The journey goes on till it meets the ocean."

As an accountant, taking stock of life and valuing it in terms of living is normal. Reconciling life with realities, situations, aspirations and writing off certain irrelevant things is essential before making a final balance sheet. When I make my balance sheet, it is ultimately a rational adjustment between ambition and achievement. The budgetary variance is normal and acceptable. However, tallying the balance sheet is a great challenge.

During this journey of seven decades in my life, I came across many crises. Crisis of conscience, crisis of confidence, crisis of moral principles and ethical practices. But I can proudly say that I have withstood the travails. It is always a battle between right and wrong. Every day it is a *Dharmakshetra*. My experience is *Dharmo Rakshati Rakshitah*, a Hindu thought, which says if you follow *Dharma, Dharma* saves you. The bible also says: You shall know the truth and the truth shall set you free.

I have grown up seeing Gandhiji's three monkeys, a plaster of paris figure on my study table. 'Do not talk bad, Do not see bad, Do not hear bad.' I think two more monkeys are required to be added i.e. 'Do not think bad and Do not do bad' That should be our *Panchasheel*.

Life has many facets. It is a combination of pleasures and pains, gains and losses, ups and downs. Opportunities do not reach the vast population in general and many are not in a position to catch them. Many talented persons in every walk of life are not in a position to pursue the opportunities due to financial reasons. For an average person, breadwinning itself is a struggle; his *Kurukshetra*. Teaching morals, telling stories is a part of our normal hypocrisy in our society. Religion only defends the social inequalities or economic disparities through Karma theory. *Dharmakshetra*'s basic rules get altered as per the situation and persons. Performing duties without expecting rewards is required as per Bhagavad Gita, however this is not possible in the present-day commercial world with a materialistic outlook. It may be achievable in social life to some extent. But life should not be a *quid pro quo*.

When we talk of the opportunities in the country with its large population in a developing country like India, equal distribution of opportunities and infrastructural facilities is difficult. The large chunk of land without irrigation facilities and drinking water makes things worse, as the country primarily depends on agriculture. I have enjoyed affluence in the irrigated areas and witnessed the total absence of it in arid regions. The successive governments made their efforts in augmenting the situation, but still a lot is to be done. The development gap results in the urbanization of population for opportunities, where many urban areas lack proper sanitation, drinking water, shelter and medical facilities. Many parents cannot afford further higher education for children as they are also immediate breadwinners. Resultantly, our country is losing many talented people. Population growth deteriorates further with socio-economic disparities widening.

I always heard that money is like salt, if you have less, it is not palatable and if it is more, it is also not desirable. That's what I was taught but it is not totally true as per my experience. In the modern days, the more money you have, the more fulfilling you feel. If you have more money, enjoy it, preserve it and invest it. With the advent of technology and globalisation, there are more opportunities and more things to give utility and pleasure. There is no limit to this happiness so long as one is not earning it at the cost of others and loss of others' prosperity. The Bible says money is the root cause of all the evils whereas Bernard Shaw says lack of money is the root cause of all evils, I tend to agree with both in two different contexts. The experience in life is not to be avaricious. Be contented, know your limitations but do your effort and duties and there is something called destiny for every person. Every person lives in this universe in a network without knowing the operator and the operation.

India could not expand its activities especially in technology-oriented sectors. Our country developed technologies over decades indigenously under the policy of self-reliance with our technical personnel including electronics, communication to even space research. By importing the gadgets, we only killed homegrown industry and technology. At present, rapid growth is possible with advanced technologies and allowing investments linked to technology.

Historical strategies like the Green revolution, the White revolution, Liberalisation, Make in India, etc have yielded good results but are not sufficient for ever-growing needs of the increasing population. There is a need to improve capital formation, increase income levels, strengthen purchasing power of the rupee, control inflation and spend on development rather than maintaining government secretariats. The overall development is possible with rapid development in technology and inviting foreign investment linked to technology since spending on research and development is low and ours is still a developing country. Reducing poverty if not eradicating it is the immediate need of the economy.

In personal life, I feel there are no other substitutes for hard work and sincerity to achieve prosperity. But ultimately what I understood is, contentment makes a person happy but it should not be synonymous for laziness or in-action. My life taught me that success is possible for people who are ready to take the opportunity and work sincerely for achieving the goals. I strongly believe that the winds and the waves are always on the side of the ablest navigators. Life is not a smooth sail.

What I have learnt in life is:
"If life is an opportunity, utilise it.
If life is a game, play it.
If life is a mistake, admit it.
If life is a struggle, fight it.
If life is a challenge, face it.
If life is interesting, enjoy it.
If life is creative, shape it.
If life is beautiful, experience it.
Live life king size. "

INDEX

D

J

K

L

M

N

O

P

R

S

T

U

V

W

Y

Z

9 789354 727283